Every Last Jew

A Teenage Boy's Story of Survival

Mark Koperweis

Published by Goff Books, an Imprint of ORO Editions.
Executive publisher: Gordon Goff.

www.goffbooks.com
info@goffbooks.com

Graphic Design: Brooke Biro
Text: Mark Koperweis
Project Coordinator: Jake Anderson

10 9 8 7 6 5 4 3 2 1 First Edition

Library of Congress data available upon request. World Rights: available.

ISBN: 978-1-943532-71-1

Color separations and printing: ORO Group Ltd.
Printed in China.

International distribution: www.goffbooks.com/distribution

Every Last Jew

A Teenage Boy's Story of Survival

 goff BOOKS

Dedicated to the memory of Zygmund, Ida, Celina, Sala, Avram, and Chaim. You will never be forgotten.

Henry at age 16. Drawing by Dana Joyce.

Without memory, there is no culture. Without memory, there would be no civilization, no society, no future.

– Elie Wiesel

Acknowledgments

I'D LIKE TO THANK, FIRST AND FOREMOST, MY FATHER HENRY for always talking about his experience. He taught us that there was something to learn from the Holocaust.

Special thanks to Cecile Moochnek who encouraged me to write; to Alan Dulfon and Mona Monfared for their excellent editing and proofreading work; to Pierre St. Clair for his sanguine advice; to Larry Brucia for asking probing questions; to Dana Joyce for her wonderful artwork; and to all my friends and family who gave me their valuable feedback and encouragement.

Every Last Jew

A Teenage Boy's Story of Survival

Preface

We often hear the imperative "Never Forget." Growing up with a father who survived the Holocaust, forgetting was never an option for me, not even for a moment. Some Holocaust survivors put their experience behind them and never mention it again because they don't want their children to have to relive what they went through. They want to insulate their children from that horrible part of their life. Not my father. Ever since I can remember, my father has been telling stories of his survival. This has created a constant background narrative in my life that I carry with me always.

When life throws its challenges at me, when bad things happen to me, when things become extremely difficult, when I am at my lowest point, my father's narrative starts playing in my head, reassuring me that whatever I am going through at the moment pales in comparison to what he went through. He never gave up; how can I? He persevered; I must. If he never lost hope, then I surely cannot. This attitude is in no way intended to trivialize the suffering of others, no matter how small physically or mentally. Everyone has their own struggles, and they are real. The point is that if you are suffering, you need strength, determination, and hope to move through the pain and come out of the other end of the tunnel of despair. My father's story provides that for me.

My entire life I have always been driven to document my father's experiences so that future generations of our family would know what he and his family went through. About twenty years ago I decided to record my father. I collected over six hours of video and audio recordings of him telling his story along with my asking him questions. It is from those recordings that I have compiled this book.

People often ask me why I feel the need to tell this story. They say that there are already so many stories published about the Holocaust, so why do we need yet another? My response is, "Six million Jews were killed. Every one of them had a story to tell. When there are six million stories published, you might have a point. It is only through the stories of those that survived that we can know the stories of those that did not."

The purpose of remembering is not to carry a life-long grudge, or to seek revenge, or to label a group of people as evil; that is what the Nazis did. A basic belief of the National Socialists was that Jews were an inferior race. They condemned an entire group of people based on nationality and ethnicity. The purpose of remembering what happened to the Jews of Europe is to learn from the past so that as a society we do not repeat our mistakes. It is for this reason that I am compelled to tell my father's particular story of survival.

I can remember writing a book report for school in fifth grade. We had to choose a non-fiction title to read. I chose *While Six Million Died* by Arthur Morse. It was one of the first books about the Holocaust and the untold story of the obstructions placed in the way of attempts to save Jews from Hitler's "Final Solution." Well, in the late Sixties no one was learning about the Holocaust in American public schools, so I'm sure that for my teacher this was an odd choice for a fifth-grader.

She asked me why I chose that particular book and I remember feeling a sense of pride when telling her that my father—*my father*—was a survivor. No other child in my entire school could make that claim about one of their parents. To me, my father was the greatest hero in the world. Six million Jews died, including many of his own family members, but somehow, he survived. That was astonishing to me, and I wanted to know how he did it. What were the circumstances which he had to endure? What was life like before his family got split up? What happened to his brothers and sisters? How did he get through it all and finally come to America? I never stopped asking my father questions, and he never tired of giving me answers.

The one question I never thought of asking until I wrote that book report in the fifth grade was the one which my teacher asked me in her final comments (after giving me an 'A')—"Why?" She wanted to know why Hitler chose the Jews as his enemy. Why was Nazi ideology inherently anti-Semitic? Why were Jews scapegoated? As a fifth-grader I couldn't answer her questions, and even today there is still no simple answer. Recently I met with a good friend for dinner and told him that I was writing this book. He told me he thought that was great because everyone's story from the Holocaust needed to be told to add to the collective memory of one of the worst periods in human history. I was delighted to hear that. It gave me a sense of encouragement to go forward.

While we were sipping our cocktails before dinner he said, "You know what I've never understood, Mark?" I shook my head. "Why the Jews? Why did Hitler and the people of Europe hate the Jews?" I took a sip of my drink and replied: "Well, that's a great question. I've been thinking about that very question since fifth grade." I then asked him: "Why do you think the Nazis used the phrase 'The Final Solution to the Jewish Question?' First, what is the question that needs an answer or solution? Second, why 'final?'" He looked puzzled and said he never really thought about that. I told him that in writing my father's story I found answers to these pressing questions and had incorporated them throughout his story. He replied, "Well, looks like I'll have to read it to find the answers." We both chuckled.

Retelling my father's story has also given me a better understanding of my people, my heritage, my culture—

where I come from and who I am. Since my mother's family were Russian Jews who came to America in the early twentieth century, this makes my Jewish origins both maternal and paternal. After writing about my father, though, I've come to identify more with my own hyphenated identity as a Jewish-American—more specifically as an Ashkenazi Jew, yet not in a religious sense but as an ethnicity. The story of the Holocaust is primarily the story of the Ashkenazim: those Jews who originally came to settle along the Rhine River in West Germany and Northern France and then moved out into the Pale of Settlement, which comprises parts of present-day Belarus, Latvia, Lithuania, Moldova, Russia, Ukraine, and my father's home country of Poland.

The Ashkenazi community was devastated throughout Europe. No family was left untouched by the killing and destruction. There were approximately 8.8 million Jews living in Europe at the beginning of World War ll. Most of them were Ashkenazi. There were 3.3 million Ashkenazi Jews living in Poland alone. Only 300,000 survived. I also came to learn that Poland had the dubious distinction of being the country with the greatest number of collaborators with the Nazis, but also the greatest number of resistance fighters during the war. They lost almost two million non-Jews fighting the Nazis.

Learning this about Poland made me realize how important it is not to generalize about any ethnicity or population of people. I have heard some members of my family say things like: "There has never been a good German, and there never will be;" or "the Poles were worse than the Nazis. They'd turn us in for a loaf of bread." While I can understand why someone would think in those terms, I've come to learn that those statements are just not true. In every culture, in every country, in every community, regardless of national origin, race, religion, gender, or skin color, there are people who sometimes act cruelly toward one another but mostly they don't. What's more, it's hard to know how we would behave if we were suddenly thrown into a horrible situation full of moral dilemmas. It's very easy to judge in hindsight, so the lesson which I've learned is to never generalize.

When I was growing up we didn't learn about the Holocaust in public school. Only my Jewish friends knew about it either from going to Hebrew school for a few hours after public school, as I did, or from their family. By the time my own kids went to public school things had changed. It seems like all children in middle school learn about the Holocaust these days. My father, who has nine grandchildren, visited most of their classrooms to discuss his experience as they learned about the Holocaust.

I remember one time when he came to King Middle School here in Berkeley to speak to my twins' class. The meeting was held in the school library and there were about three classes assembled there. When my father walked in, the entire room of people stood up and gave him a standing ovation before he'd said a single word. He spoke for a few minutes and then took questions from the kids. At one point they asked to see the number tattooed on his arm and the scar on his back from being stabbed by a Nazi soldier. That was a very proud moment both for me and for my twins. We took pride in his survival.

My father is now 92 and no longer gives talks in classrooms. Soon he and the rest of the handful of survivors who are out there will be gone, and I've thought about the effect that will have on Holocaust education around the world. In just another decade or so there will be no more eyewitnesses to the tragedy, so I decided that the next best thing to an actual survivor telling their story is the child of that survivor telling it. That is why I formed a non-profit organization, The Henry Koperweis Foundation for Holocaust Education.

The mission of the foundation is to promote an awareness of the atrocities committed by the Nazis against the Jews of Europe through the personal story of my father. By bringing a short multimedia presentation to a classroom and having a question-and-answer period, young students can potentially be connected to what happened in a more visceral way and better understand how they can learn from it. It is my hope that this book can be used as a tool for young students to read and discuss in a group setting. For example, teachers and educators could present a set of questions that each student could answer and discuss based on my father's story, which represents the story of millions who did not survive.

In spite of all the documentation and personal testimony that exists today regarding the Holocaust, there are still people who want to deny that it happened or rewrite history, saying that it was an exaggeration or that it was not the intention of the Nazis to exterminate European Jewry. Holocaust denial takes many forms, yet nothing combats denial of an event better than the testimony of one who experienced it firsthand. Hearing my father's story counteracts this denial and also serves as an example of what can happen in human society when racial prejudices are tolerated, or worse still, promoted. It also highlights the danger of propaganda and reinforces the need for every individual to develop critical thinking skills in order to be vigilant in detecting and fighting racism, prejudice, and bigotry wherever and whenever this three-headed snake spews its insidious venom.

I can never fully comprehend what it was like for my father as a young teenager being torn away from his friends and family and all that was normal for him. I can't fathom what it was like not knowing when or if your struggle would end. It's inconceivable, and equally incomprehensible to think about how many lives were lost. To get a grasp of the enormity of the loss of life, consider this: If you held a minute of silence for every person who perished in the Holocaust, you would remain silent for eleven years. Although there is certainly a time for silence, there's also a time for speaking up, and this book is the latter.

Thank you in advance for taking the time to read my father's account of one of the darkest, most hateful periods in human history. A great deal of progress has been made since that time. People are more tolerant and accepting of others and have come to realize that no matter what one's ethnic, religious, or cultural background, we are all part of one race, the human race. This, too, we should never forget.

Chapter 1
Kilinskiego 11

HENRY SHARED A SINGLE BED WITH HIS TWO YOUNGER brothers, Avram and Chaim, in a three-bedroom flat in a run-down brick building in Radom, Poland. His Polish name was Hennek, but his family called him by his Yiddish name, Haskel. His three older brothers, Harry (Herschel), Julius, and Joe (Yasel), along with their sister Celina, shared another bedroom; and his mother and father were in the third. His oldest sister Sala was already married and living with her husband Moishe a short distance away. Henry woke up early one day so that he and his brother Harry could get fresh milk from the market. He washed his face in a basin in the foyer next to his room and then put on his clothes, making sure not to forget his white armband with a blue Star of David in the center. His father, Zygmund, was at his sewing machine in their living room, which doubled as a tailor shop. His mother Ida was busy preparing breakfast. There was a small container of milk sitting on the window sill. It had been there for a few days curdling into buttermilk.

Together, Henry and his older brother Harry carried a large five-gallon aluminum container as they walked to the marketplace. They passed businesses and shops that had paper signs posted on them letting the public know that they were owned by Jews. As they made their way to the market they were careful not to walk on the sidewalk, as it was forbidden for a Jew to do so. Instead, they walked in the street alongside the curb paying particular attention so as not to be struck by a vehicle. After they got the milk, it took all of their strength and dexterity to carry it back without spilling any. There was a small storage area in the basement of the apartment that was allotted to their family to store their groceries to keep them fresh, but there was no refrigerator. They struggled down the few steps to the cellar and placed the container in its usual spot. Herschel grabbed a ladle that was hanging on a hook, opened the lid of the container, scooped out some milk, and carefully filled a bowl to bring upstairs.

When they came upstairs their mother Ida had breakfast prepared: hot cereal and fresh bread. There was no juice, as that was a luxury. The only time they had juice was when one of them was sick. It served as medicine. Ida began serving the cereal as the whole family sat at the breakfast table together. It had been several months since the Germans announced that all Jews were forbidden to go to public school. They even closed all Hebrew schools. Before this happened, Henry would typically pack his small tin with lunch after eating breakfast, and accompanied by his siblings he would walk to school nearby. After school let out at 2:30 he and his siblings would walk back home and snack on fruit and cookies. Henry would then head off to Hebrew school for two more hours along with all three of his older brothers. There they learned how to read and write Hebrew, as well as how to *daven* or recite passages from the *Chumash*, the Five Books of Moses. After Hebrew school the whole family would eat dinner together and then Henry would go do his school reading assignments. His older sister Celina would sometimes help him.

As Henry sat with his family eating a modest breakfast, he remembered how, just a few months ago, when he turned thirteen he had his Jewish coming of age ritual, his bar mitzvah. In order to prepare for the event, he had been visiting his grandfather, Herschel Bayer, at his home nearby. Hashbayer, as Henry called him, was a very learned man. He had a long white beard and always wore a yarmulke atop his white head of hair. He would sit sternly and listen to Henry recite his *Haftarah*, a series of selections from the Book of the Twelve Prophets of the Hebrew Bible, correcting him when necessary on his pronunciation and singing. It was customary for a young man to learn a particular *Haftarah* and recite it as part of the bar mitzvah ritual. Hashbayer was like a rabbi to Henry. After his lesson, Hashbayer would give Henry a hug, tell him that he was doing a great job, and give him a piece of chocolate. He would then go into a lengthy exegesis on the meaning of the Hebrew passages he had just recited, which Hashbayer knew by heart. These days Henry was no longer able to go to Hebrew school, or any school for that matter, because the Germans forbade it, but he did still manage to visit his scholarly grandfather on occasion.

After breakfast Henry spent his day playing soccer with his brothers and his Polish friends, Yanek and Benyek, when they got home from school. Henry had his own soccer ball that was a gift for his eleventh birthday, yet he owned little else in the form of toys. He dreamed of playing as a professional someday.

Soon it was time for dinner. His father was still working in the living room on his tailoring while his mother prepared dinner in their tiny kitchen. Zygmund was an optimistic man—hard working, stern, deeply religious and orthodox. He kept the home kosher, went to the synagogue on the Sabbath, and observed the High Holy Days. Oddly, the boycott of Jewish businesses didn't affect his business. Henry would often see German soldiers in his living room standing at attention while his father would take precise measurements in order to make custom civilian suits for them which they would somehow send back to Germany. They would pay him a decent amount and sometimes they would even bring him bread, sugar, kielbasa, or chocolate. The German Wehrmacht (armed forces) had closed a school across the street and was using it as their headquarters. Word spread quickly among them about Zygmund's sartorial skills, and as a result he was very busy.

After dinner Henry kicked around his soccer ball in the courtyard for a while and then came in to get ready for bed. Shortly after washing his face he came to say good night to his mother and father, whom he addressed as Mama and Tata, respectively. Seeing him, his father smiled and addressed him as Haskela, the "a" at the end of his name adding an extra shade of affection. "Come here, my son," he said, stretching out his arms from behind his sewing machine. Henry walked over with his soccer ball under one arm. His father gave him a kiss and a big hug. As he rubbed Henry's head, he exhaled heavily, "Time for bed, my son. Get some rest. Tomorrow's another day. A better day. Soon, when all of this is over, life will be better, my boy. I'll sit in a stadium filled with thousands of cheering fans and watch you kick that ball down the field to score a goal as the crowd goes wild. Someday, my boy. In the meantime, get some rest, no?" He went back to work as Henry walked to his room. He placed his football underneath his bed, talked with his siblings for a while, and then turned in for the evening.

In the dead of night Henry was suddenly awakened, along with everyone else in the house. *Thump, thump, thump.* Someone was pounding on the front door.

"Jude, raus, raus. Schnell, schnell!" ("Jew, out, out. Quickly, quickly!"), a German soldier was shouting through the door.

"What in God's name is going on?" Zygmund cried out as he hurried to open the door before it was knocked down by the pounding.

"Coming, coming." Zygmund opened the door. Two German soldiers with machine guns and German Shepherds along with an SS officer (of the Schutzstaffel, the "Protection Squadron") stood at the front door and began barking out orders to the horrified family inside.

"You have ten minutes," the officer began. "Take only what you can carry and come outside. You're being moved to Glinice." The officer and soldiers turned away and walked to the next door.

"What's going on, Zygmund?" Ida asked with tears in her eyes. "What do they mean we're being moved?"

"For how long? And why?" asked Henry's older sister Celina.

"Listen, listen," Zygmund said, trying to calm everyone down. "I don't know, but we better do what they say. They have machine guns, for God's sake!"

"How can this be happening, Zygmund? What did we do?" Henry's mother cried out as she quickly went into her bedroom to gather some belongings. "Why, God? Why?" she uttered, throwing her hands up.

Everyone started frantically collecting items to take with them. Henry went back into his bedroom and looked around for things to bring: some shirts, underwear, a couple of pairs of trousers, his football. Just then his father came into the room with a large bundle.

"Here," he handed the bundle to Henry, "I need you to carry this for your little brothers and your sister. It has all their clothes for the next few days until we can figure out what's going on here." His father left the room in a panic.

A terrible feeling settled in Henry's stomach as he gathered his belongings. Realizing that his hands would be too full to carry his soccer ball, he pushed it under his bed to hide it. Maybe he would be able to come back to get it later.

"Haskel," his mother called out to Henry. "Let's go, sweetheart." Henry quickly left his room.

On his way out, he noticed some clothes hanging on the rack next to his father's sewing machine. It was yesterday's completed work. "What will happen to it now?" he thought to himself. A pair of trousers was lying next to the machine on the table, waiting to be repaired. A small piece of paper was pinned to one of the legs with a name written on it. "How will the owner get them back?" he wondered. He looked into the kitchen. The pots and pans that his mother had just cleaned after dinner earlier that night were hanging above the stove. He caught a glimpse of his room through the open door.

His soccer ball had rolled out from under the bed and was in the middle of the room. Henry quickly ran over and grabbed it clumsily.

He ran outside to catch up with his family. Soldiers with dogs and SS officers were directing crowds over to covered trucks idling behind them in a long single file. Lights were glaring in Henry's eyes, making it hard to see. He noticed other Jewish neighbors being led onto trucks while they carried their bundles. He wondered what his friends were able to bring and what they had to leave behind. He looked up, across the courtyard, to his Polish friends' houses. Their doors were all closed, but he noticed people peeking out from behind their curtains—watching, just watching, in what Henry perceived to be a kind of silent approval. "Why don't they say something?" he thought to himself. "Maybe they're just as scared as we are," he thought.

Henry looked and saw his Polish friends Yanek and Benyek looking out of their windows. They had just played soccer together earlier that day. They both stared at him as a soldier yelled, "Schnell, schnell," and pushed Henry in the back with his rifle butt. Henry dropped his ball as he ran to catch up with the rest of his family. He would have to leave it behind. His mother was holding his two younger brothers by their hands as they cried and trembled. Zygmund was trying to keep track of everyone amidst the commotion.

They climbed into one of the trucks lined up in the street. Lights were glaring. Engines were running. The inside of the truck was dark, cold, musty. There were no seats. They all had to stand. The truck filled up. An officer yelled and the truck started moving. Everyone jerked back, then forward. Babies were crying with grimaced faces. Mothers were wiping tears from their babies' eyes. Husbands were comforting their wives with hugs. Henry looked back and saw the truck behind him being loaded with more of his Jewish neighbors. They all climbed into their truck clutching their pathetic bundles. All of their life's possessions were reduced to a small satchel packed in fear and desperation.

As the truck drove away carrying Henry and his family, he caught a glimpse of a German soldier kicking a soccer ball down the street in the direction of their truck while shouting, "Alle Jude, raus!" ("All Jews, get out!") A group of German soldiers laughed as the ball rolled against the curb, coming to a gradual stop. Henry's heart sank deep into his stomach. The ball was motionless and alone. The truck kept moving. A sickening silence settled in.

Chapter 2
The Ghetto

WHEN THE TRUCK PULLED UP TO GLINICE STREET CARRYING Henry and his family, he noticed that there was a tall, long fence made from wooden poles and barbed wire running across the street, flanked by rows of old apartment buildings. There appeared to be only one entrance. Above the gate there was a sign that read: *Danger of Contamination—Do Not Enter!*

Henry used to pass this street often. Every week someone in the family had to go to the kosher butcher to have a live chicken killed for the Sabbath meal. Just last week it was Henry's turn. He remembered how he tried to hold the chicken steady while he was waiting for his turn to get to the butcher. He tried holding it down with his foot, but the chicken quickly got away and started running down the street. Henry knew that if the chicken escaped, his parents would be extremely upset, so he ran after it in earnest. He finally cornered the bird in an alley. After a brief ordeal of being pecked several times, he was able to grab it. As he brought the chicken back to meet its destiny he passed by this very same street.

Even though Henry was hardly living in luxury at Kilinskiego Street, he did notice that Glinice was old, run-down, filthy, and extremely crowded with destitute-looking people. It was clearly the poor side of town where only gentile Poles used to live. No Jews. Now, while arriving on this truck at the break of dawn, Henry thought to himself, "Where are all the gentiles who used to live here?" He couldn't help but wonder if they were all now living in his house. "Maybe this is what happens during wartime," he wondered. The truck pulled through the gate. Henry noticed the shocked look on his parents' faces. He turned to his father who was holding his sleeping brother, Chaim, in his arms.

"Papa," he began with a puzzled look on his face. "Why are we here? What's going on?"

"Don't worry, Haskel," his father encouraged him. "It's this stupid war. We'll know more later."

His father rubbed Chaim's head to wake him up. The sun was just peeking over the horizon. Henry was reminded of how his father used to wake him up every day in his bed by rubbing his head. It was just about the same time of morning. His mother Ida would already be up cooking cereal for the whole family. She would buy fresh bread at the market every day, and they would drink the raw milk that they kept in the cellar below the house in a large metal milk container. Sometimes they had some of the buttermilk that she made by keeping some milk on the window sill inside the house and letting the sun curdle it slightly. They would all eat together. But today that would not be happening. No one knew what would be happening.

The truck came to a sudden stop. Everyone lunged forward, then back. A German soldier opened the back of the truck and ordered everyone out. Henry and his family were assigned an apartment to go to. It was one room, and all eight of them were to live there. They brought all their things inside the room. It was empty, save for a few pots, a bucket, and a tiny worn cot. They stood there in disbelief. Ida dropped her bundle and began to weep, "Why, God? Why?" Zygmund walked over and held her. "He hasn't forgotten us. This won't last long," he whispered as everyone stood motionless, wondering, scared.

The next morning at 7:00 a.m. all the inhabitants of the Glinice ghetto, about two thousand people, gathered at designated areas to be fed. There was very little food allowed into the ghetto—cereal, some potatoes, beans, and sometimes a little butter. A group of Jews appointed by the Germans called the Judenrat (Council of Jews) were essentially the administrators of the ghetto. They organized the medical clinics, the food distribution, and all the dealings with the Germans. After eating a small breakfast, a truck took Henry and his two older brothers Joe and Harry to a nearby camp in Wolanow to work for the Germans. No one was allowed to work inside the ghetto, and no one could leave or enter the ghetto gates on their own.

*   *   *   *   *

Several months had passed. It was the summer of 1942. Henry and his family were asleep in their one-room apartment. There were some mattresses on the floor to form a large bed along with some blankets and pillows. Henry and Harry had worked all day, for twelve hours, at Wolanow. Harry hadn't come home that night but was sleeping in the barracks that they were building at the camp. Before going to bed, Zygmund asked Henry what kind of work he was doing and how he was being treated by the Germans. They never talked about what was going on in the ghetto or when it would end; they simply had silent hope that somehow things would change for the better. Maybe the war would end and they would go back to their home. For now, at least they were together, except for Julius, Henry's oldest brother, who had gone off to Russia with his employer.

Julius's boss owned a coffee roasting company, and being Jewish as well, he had suspicions that things were only going to get worse for Jews after the Germans occupied Poland in 1939. A year ago, when they were both still living in their homes on Kilinskiego Street, Julius's boss came to Henry's house with a car. He talked

33

to Henry's mother and father for a few minutes and told them that it was just a matter of time before the Germans would make life very difficult for Jews. He feared for his safety and for all of the Jews in Poland. Henry heard him say something about how he knew someone in Russia and that he wanted to go there and bring Julius with him. He assured them that life would be better and safer there. Henry's parents reluctantly agreed. Henry stood in the courtyard watching as his parents hugged Julius while his boss waited in the car for him. Carrying a small suitcase, Julius got in the car and waved goodbye to his parents as the car drove off. They had no idea if they would ever see each other again. Zygmund put his arm around his wife's shoulders and walked her back into the house as she cried.

Now, as Henry's family slept, the entire ghetto was being surrounded by German soldiers. He had trouble sleeping remembering that his brother Herschel told him the day before that the Germans were planning on moving everyone from the ghetto and deporting them to camps in the countryside. Henry didn't want to take him seriously but couldn't help thinking that it might be true. There were no newspapers or radio in the ghetto so rumors about what was going on would spread every day. "Was this just another rumor, or could Herschel be right?" Henry wondered while he tried to fall asleep.

He stared at the streams of light coming through the window, streaking the ceiling with fixed, intricate vertical patterns. He asked himself, "What's next? The German soldiers took our home away and crowded us into this tiny room to live on top of one another. They feed us a small amount of food, keep us from going to school, prevent my father from working, and force my brothers and I to work with almost no pay, every day, like slaves. What's next?"

Just then Henry heard some trucks pull up outside. Beams of light from their headlamps swept across the ceiling, displacing the patterns he was looking at. He peeked out of the window. German soldiers were getting out of their trucks with rifles and machine guns. Fear filled Henry's entire body. Blood rushed to his head as he woke everyone up. "They're back. They're here, get up!" he exclaimed in a panic. Henry looked out of the window again as everyone began waking up. He saw German soldiers with their ubiquitous German Shepherds starting to fill the streets of the ghetto. As the soldiers began banging on doors, lights started turning on inside peoples' rooms. People were being dragged from their rooms and made to line up outside.

Suddenly, before Henry could react to what he was seeing, there was a pounding at the door. German soldiers were yelling, "Jude raus!" ("Jew out!") His mother screamed as his father opened the door, and instantly he was pulled out of the room. The soldiers ordered everyone out. His mother helped his younger brothers out of the room. As they got outside, an SS officer directed people with the wave of his hand to either keep moving on the line to the right or to wait on the line to the left. Henry noticed that the people on the line to the right were waiting at the nearby train station where there were freight cars being filled with people. He heard gunfire and quickly turned. An old man fell to the ground. Another shot was fired. A woman went down near him. People were panicked. Some were hiding under cars or around buildings. He saw them getting dragged into the street and shot. Mothers were weeping as their children were forcibly ripped from their arms.

Henry and his family reached the SS officer. He waved his hand for Henry, Joe, and Zygmund to stay in the line to the left. They were to get on an open truck. Henry's mother, along with his two younger brothers Chaim and Avram as well as his older sister Celina, were waved to the right to move toward the train. Noticing this, Zygmund yelled out to Henry through the tumult, "I have to go be with your mother and the younger kids. You stay here." Zygmund turned and was instantly caught up in the crowd. Henry quickly lost sight of him. "Papa," he yelled, to no avail. Henry felt the butt of a machine gun pressing hard into his back, forcing him to stay in his line. He almost tripped over something on the ground and looked down. An old man with a beard was lying face down in a puddle of blood. "Don't resist," he whispered to himself. "Keep moving and you'll be okay."

He was loaded onto a truck with his older brother Joe and about fifty other people. He looked back into the crowd trying desperately to find his parents and siblings in the mass of hysterical people. He caught a glimpse of them being forced onto the train. His father had reached the others and was looking back toward the truck that Henry and Joe were now on. Henry had no idea if he would ever see them again. Henry and his older brother were now alone, surrounded by disillusioned strangers sharing a common yet unknown dismal future. The truck pulled away. Henry covered his face with his hands and wept as Joe patted him on the head.

Chapter 3
Every Last Jew

HENRY SLOWLY OPENED THE HOLSTER HOLDING THE LUGER as his heart pounded. He anxiously looked back at the door of the barracks to see if the Obersturmbannfuhrer (Lieutenant Colonel) was approaching. The gun felt cold and heavy in his hand. Henry was familiar with the sight and sound of this particular weapon although he never held one in his hands. He had heard it fired and had seen the damage it was capable of. This particular gun belonged to Obersturmbannfuhrer Baumann. Henry was assigned the tasks of shining Baumann's boots and leather holster, mending his uniforms, straightening his quarters, and even cleaning his gun—the gun he was now holding for the first time, which was beckoning him to take action.

His mind started racing with ideas of waiting for Baumann to walk through the door and shooting him in the face. "I should kill that bastard," he thought to himself. "He won't know what hit him. I'll show him who's in charge. Then I'll run outside and kill as many rotten, goddam Nazis as I can before the guards in the towers shoot me dead. Everyone will watch with awe and disbelief. I'll die a hero, on my terms, and not at the whim of a Nazi who takes pleasure in killing Jews. That son of a bitch, Baumann—I'll show him!"

Just then the door flung open. Henry was startled. He quickly turned his head toward the door. It was Baumann, who stopped for a brief moment and was also slightly startled to see someone in his quarters. Henry's heart was racing as a flash of blood filled his head with a warm wave of fear. Baumann appeared to Henry as a towering figure slightly silhouetted by the daylight behind him. He was wearing his full green-gray uniform, replete with epaulettes, medallions, and badges, including the all-pervasive haunting swastika. His tall black, well-polished boots and officer's cap added to his intimidating air of authority. Henry was momentarily paralyzed in fear.

Seeing Henry, a boy barely 15 years old, standing motionless, holding his sidearm, Baumann smiled. Henry was both relieved and confused. "Be careful, that's loaded, my boy; you could hurt yourself," Baumann said jokingly. Henry turned and placed the gun back in its holster, breathing a silent sigh of relief. "I should've shot the bastard," he thought, feeling somewhat disappointed in himself. "But then what? What would I have gained? Do I really want to die? I want to find out what happened to the rest of my family. Are they still alive? Are they in a camp similar to this one? If they had this chance, would they have the audacity to shoot a Nazi officer? Or would they push on, hoping their struggle would soon end and they would be free?"

Baumann walked over to Henry and put his hand on his shoulder. "You know, Henry, I like you," he said with a commanding voice. "You're a good Jew. I will kill every last Jew on Earth, Henry, but you...you I will spare. All the others will die. Only you will survive." Baumann looked at Henry with a reassuring smile as he patted him on the head. Henry felt incredibly scared, but at the same time invincible. He felt as though he would not die, that he would survive no matter what. He looked up on the wall at the holster holding Baumann's Luger that he was holding just a few seconds earlier. "Killing him would have surely meant killing myself," he thought.

There was an announcement over the loudspeakers to line up outside. "Looks like it's time to go," Baumann said while waving his hand toward the doorway. Henry hurried outside as all the men began gathering. He saw his brothers Joe and Harry. They all lined up together. It only took a few minutes for all two thousand men at the Wolanow camp to assemble in one spot. "We need some of you to go work in Radom at a munitions factory," Bauman said while walking slowly down the rows of men, deciding who to choose. When he reached Henry, he stopped for a moment. "Sorry, my boy. I won't be able to use you here anymore. You're going back to Radom," he informed Henry, and then moved on to his two brothers. When Henry saw Baumann walk past them his heart became heavy with fear and sadness realizing that he was now going to be separated from the only two other family members in his life.

"It's just for a while, right?" Henry asked his brothers.

"Yes, yes," Joe assured him. "We won't be split up for long. Besides, you get to go back to our home town. Who knows, maybe you'll meet someone you know at the factory and they'll give you some extra food."

"Don't worry, we will see you soon. Be strong," Harry reassured his younger brother while giving him a quick pat on the back.

"See you soon, Hennek," Joe said affectionately as he and Harry walked toward their barracks. Neither of them looked back.

Henry stood there for a few seconds taking in the last moments of being with his two older brothers. As he watched them walk away he looked around. Men were frantically gathering their few belongings from the endless rows of barracks and were then getting into their respective trucks. The main gates to the camp were open. The guards in their watchtowers tightly gripped their machine guns. Henry realized how diabolically clever the Germans were when they first took over Poland, his home. He and his brothers were forced to work in this camp over a year ago. The Germans told them they were building barracks for the army. They even got paid a little bit and were still living with their parents in the ghetto. But for the past several months it had been Henry and his brothers' prison, built with their own hands, holding them against their will.

Henry ran into his barrack and grabbed his things and then went outside where he was directed to a truck that would take him back to Radom. As he sat waiting for the truck to depart, his mind was filled with thoughts of the day he was torn away from his mother and father, his two younger brothers, and his older sister when the ghetto was liquidated about a year ago. At that time he was loaded onto a similar truck, almost exactly the same as the one he was now on. In fact, it could have been the same one; he couldn't tell. He wasn't even sure how much time had passed since then. "Was it one year ago, or was it two?" he asked himself. "Was it months, or years?" He couldn't answer.

As terrible as this place in Wolanow had been, he realized that he had become oddly accustomed to it. He felt a sadness about leaving and an uncertainty about his future. He was being torn from his remaining family members. "What will it be like without them?" he thought. "Who will look out for me? Will I ever see them again?" Henry looked out into the forest. It seemed so peaceful and picturesque. On a different day, under different circumstances one would be inspired by the natural beauty that surrounded him. He watched birds flying in and out of trees, singing to one another. "They don't even realize that they are free," he thought to himself. "If I could change places with them, I would do it in a second."

As the truck began moving, Henry looked back at the camp. All he could see were rows of trucks being filled with young men just like himself—scared, heartbroken, sad, confused, and most of all, angry. The orange glow of the setting sun caught Henry's eye as it reflected off the neatly polished, black leather holster strapped to Baumann's hip, holding his Luger. As the Obersturmbannfuhrer waved his hand this way and that, directing men to their designated trucks, Henry could hear his haunting voice in his head as he watched him shrink in the distance: "Only you will survive, my boy. Only you will survive!"

Chapter 4

Combs for Kielbasa

MAKING FIVE HUNDRED RIFLE BARREL TIPS PER DAY WAS NO easy task. Any mistakes and you could be taken outside and shot. This was Henry's job while he was forced to work at the munitions factory just outside Radom. What once produced bicycles was now converted into a production line to feed the Nazi war machine with rifles and pistols. Henry worked alongside Polish civilians who were hired by the Nazis to work there, yet he was not as fortunate as they were. He had to work twelve-hour days in exchange for a pathetic amount of food and the privilege of staying alive.

Every morning Henry and several hundred other Jewish prisoners would march from the Konzentrationslager (concentration camp), the KL near Radom, to the munitions factory about an hour away. When he first arrived by truck along with hundreds of other men, he found the KL surrounded by tall barbed-wire fences. The men were split into many small groups: there were Jews, Mongols, Tatars, Russians, and Yugoslavians. The Nazis considered them all to be political prisoners, and so they had to take off all of their clothes and shoes and remove all of their jewelry, including eyeglasses. Henry's head was shaved, and he was given a blue and gray striped uniform with a small round cap and a pair of black shoes. A patch was sewn on his uniform just above the left breast in the shape of a red triangle designating him as a political prisoner. He wondered why he, a boy of 15, was now a political prisoner. "Maybe these other people are political prisoners," he thought to himself angrily. "My only crime is being Jewish!" He only had this one uniform to wear day and night. If he wanted to wash it, he did it by hand at night and slept naked on a wooden bunk bed that had some straw scattered on it for a mattress. Or sometimes he just wore it wet all day until it dried.

He was given a metal bowl and a spoon. These were his only possessions. He kept them with him at all times because if he lost his bowl, he would not eat. Therefore it became the most valuable possession in his life. He was fed once a day, after working for twelve hours in the munitions factory. His meal consisted of a thin soup—mostly water with a few small pieces of potato at the bottom—and a tiny piece of bread.

Henry was now separated from his entire family, yet he seldom thought of them. He was too hungry and caught up in the immediate need for survival. He knew that the only way he could continue to live was to get some extra food from the Poles who worked at the factory alongside him. He saw grown men slowly whittle away, day by day.

They would get weaker and thinner until they would just drop dead. He didn't want to wind up like that. He didn't want to starve. He didn't want to be hungry all the time, which he was. His mind was filled with thoughts of how to obtain food from the Poles without getting shot, and this kept his mind from wondering what happened to his parents and siblings. His family became secondary. His primary goal was food.

At the factory he was assigned to a foreman who showed him what his tasks would be. One machine was cutting large tubes into smaller ones. A second machine was threading the small tubes. A third would shave some of the ends off. A fourth would make even finer cuts. The fifth would polish the final piece. All of these machines were set on automatic and were calibrated to run at a particular rate to produce his quota of five hundred pieces per day. He had three Jewish friends who he knew growing up who now worked with him: Felix, Walter, and Jacob. Felix's job was to clean up all of the metal scraps that would fall to the factory floor. He would take them to an area where they were melted down and recycled back into raw material. Jacob's job was to keep all of the machine operators supplied with the specific parts they needed. All day he would go from the supply area and make his rounds to all of the machine operators, including Henry. Walter ran another set of machines similar to Henry's.

In a matter of days Henry had figured out that if he put the machines on manual, he could run them faster and get his daily quota done in only ten hours. This would leave him spare time to manufacture some combs and small brass rings that he could give to the Poles working there in exchange for food that they would bring from home: bread, butter, eggs, and if he was lucky, some kielbasa. The problem was that when Henry put the machines on manual to make them run faster, some of the parts would break. He had a small limit of acceptable broken parts. If he exceeded the allotted amount it would be considered sabotage and he would certainly be shot. "I have to figure out a way to dispose of the broken parts," he thought to himself. "There's no way I'm going to last on the food the Nazis are giving me. These Poles could help me if they wanted to. They could bring me some clothes from home and I could take off this striped uniform, put on a hat, and walk right out of here at the end of the day." Henry knew that this was unfortunately not going to happen, so he came up with a plan.

Whenever he broke a part from running the machines too fast, he would hide it and give it to Felix to dispose of when he came around to pick up the scraps from the floor. The trick was to keep track of the specific part that broke and to know exactly how many. He would then make sure that Jacob would steal those parts from the supply room and replenish Henry's supply when he came back around. Henry had to be extra careful because a Polish supervisor would come around periodically to check on all of the workers, and if he noticed anything suspicious he would report it to his Nazi superior. Henry got so good at running the machines on manual that he had two to three hours each day to make aluminum combs and brass rings. The Poles loved them and gave him a steady supply of food that they would sneak in with their lunch. Henry, Felix, Walter, and Jacob would keep the food in their pockets and quickly eat it when no one was watching, because if any of them were caught, it would be the last meal of their lives.

One day Henry approached one of the Polish civilian workers named Stachek who was a big shot on the production floor. "You know, before the Germans came," Henry started, "we were all living in peace, and things were good between us. Would it be so terrible if you gave me some food without me having to risk my life trading you something for it?" Stachek looked Henry straight in the face and replied, "Too bad, Jew-boy," and walked away. Henry decided at that moment to never expect any help from the hired Poles without having to give them something in return. He knew that they were indoctrinated by Nazi propaganda, and so he started fearing that one of them might even turn him in. He knew many Poles who were convinced that the Jew was a lesser human being, a poison in society that was destroying their culture and ruining their country.

Henry had heard that Poles would turn escaped Jews in for a loaf of bread or some butter, so he was convinced that there was no way any Pole was going to help him unless he gave them something they needed.

*   *   *   *   *

One year had passed since Henry first arrived at the KL. He was awakened early in the morning and was told that he was not going to the munitions factory to work any longer. Instead, he and a few thousand other men would be marching to Tomaszow, a small town over one hundred kilometers away. They were told that they were being moved to another camp to work. Thousands of men lined up in neat rows. They walked three abreast in the street while German soldiers flanked them on foot and on horses. They had nothing but the striped uniforms on their backs and their only other possessions in the world, their spoon and bowl. No one had any idea how long the march would take or when they would get to rest or eat.

After walking all day, they stopped in an open field to spend the night. They hadn't eaten all day and no one knew when they would. Everyone was told to lie down on the ground and go to sleep. They were exhausted from the march and welcomed the earth as their bed. While Henry was sleeping he was awakened by the sound of several men whispering. Three brothers were frantically digging a hole in the ground with their spoons and bowls. They were far enough in the crowd of several thousand men that the German soldiers on the outskirts could not notice them. They dug all night. In the morning when Henry woke up he noticed that one of the brothers was missing. His two brothers buried him in that hole with a piece of straw sticking up for him to breathe through. Everyone lined back up to continue their march. The Germans had no way of knowing if anyone was missing, and when the group was far away, the man dug himself out and escaped.

Henry wondered how that man would be able to get away. After all, he had a shaved head and was wearing a striped prisoner's uniform. It reminded Henry of the time that he had escaped when he was being held at Wolanow and was working with his brothers Joe and Harry building barracks for the Germans. At that time he didn't have a shaved head or a uniform. He noticed a gap in one of the fences in the camp. There was a small road next to the camp and a farmer lived across the street with his family. One day Henry was able to slip under the fence and run across the road without any of the German guards noticing him. He ran to the farmer's house and pleaded with him to take him in as one of his children. It would have been easy enough because he already had eight or nine of them, and Henry had heard of Jewish children who were living with Poles. The farmer was scared, however, and told Henry that if he got caught, the Germans would kill him and his family. He told Henry to leave at once. Not knowing where to go or where to hide, Henry decided that it would be better for him to go back before anyone knew he was gone. He ran back to the breach in the fence and snuck back into the camp unnoticed.

The group walked until nightfall for the second day and approached a large building that was used as a tannery. There was a smell of flesh in the air, and Henry had heard rumors that the Germans were killing Jews by gassing them in large rooms that appeared to be showers. Fear filled his entire being as he thought that these were his last moments. He was sure that he would die this night. The group was commanded to halt by a German officer, Obersturmbannfuhrer Katzmann, who came riding up atop a beautifully groomed horse. "My orders are to take all of you to Auschwitz," he began in his deep German voice. "Do not be afraid; this building was being used as a tannery and that is why it smells the way it does. We will sleep here tonight. Tomorrow you will be put on a train. To show you that it is safe I will personally stay here with you." He proceeded to ride his horse to the warehouse, where he dismounted and went inside. Seeing this Henry felt some relief and went inside with thousands of other men.

After being fed a tiny ration of soup and bread, all the men prepared for sleep. The building was uncomfortably hot and the odor was overpowering. Exhausted from a day of non-stop walking, Henry gladly dropped down to the ground to get some rest. "So they're not going to kill us here," he thought to himself, lying on the ground and staring at the ceiling which hung far above him. "They're taking us to Auschwitz to finish us all off." Henry didn't want to believe it. He tried to convince himself that what he had heard were indeed only rumors. He wondered what it would be like to asphyxiate in a gas chamber. He imagined the horror and panic of hundreds of men trapped in a large room as noxious gas filled their lungs, slowly rendering them unconscious as they fell into a permanent slumber. His eyes then closed and he fell deep asleep.

Chapter 5
Angel of Death

It had been almost two days since Henry had any food or water. After marching for almost three days from Radom to Tomaszow he was transported by bus and then loaded onto a freight train with thousands of other men. Everyone was packed so tight into the freight cars that they held each other up like manikins stuffed into a storage closet. Perhaps fifty people could fit comfortably in the car Henry occupied. There must have been nearly two hundred. If anyone had to relieve themselves along the grueling journey, there was no other option but to do so where they stood. There was a small bucket that served as a latrine, but it was impossible to find or get to in the overpacked car. The smell of urine and human waste was overwhelming. It was physically impossible to sit or lie down. Almost no light entered the car except for a small ventilation window in the top corner which allowed a narrow beam of sunlight to stream in, revealing the misery inside.

The train finally crept to a halt. When it lurched, everyone moved like one solid mass, each body feeling the weight of the entire crowd. Suddenly the large door rolled open and blinding daylight flooded in. Henry shielded his face from the sun while his eyes adjusted to the intense light of the outdoors. As people started getting off the train, many bodies just fell to the floor of the train as space opened up and the crowd could no longer hold them up. As Henry slowly moved toward the door, he noticed that his older cousin Leon had been in the train car with him. They hadn't seen each other in years, but Henry felt relieved that he was with a fellow family member. It made him feel as if he were not alone. Since Leon was several years older, Henry looked up to him as if he were another older brother. With the little bit of energy they had left in them, Henry and Leon got down from the train. Several bodies fell out of the train and were piled up below them. They tried to avoid hitting them when they jumped out of the train car.

As Henry looked around in confusion he saw thousands of people disembarking from different cars of the train. A long, narrow area in front of the train tracks was packed with civilians holding their only belongings in the world, all contained in small leather valises. All the men were separated from the women and children. Guards with machine guns were directing people to line up in neat, orderly rows. About 200 yards from where Henry was standing, at the end of a long stretch of railroad tracks, he could see a large, wide building—the entrance to Auschwitz.

A truck packed with small crying children came into Henry's view. On top of the truck on a tiny platform was a band comprised of prisoners playing loud music as if to drown out the sounds of terror coming from below. Shocked and in utter disbelief Henry and Leon watched as the truck drove past them toward the rows of endless barracks bordered by two consecutive rows of extremely tall electrified fences. At the top of each fence barbed wire was strung across thick wooden posts that curved inward like so many trained cobras guarding a fortress. In front of these barracks and out of Henry's sight was a tall iron gate that rose over a small dirt road. Along the curved top of the wrought iron arch in large letters was the insidious phrase "ARBEIT MACHT FREI" ("Work sets you free"). Rising above all the buildings, far in the background, were two tall rectangular towers billowing a constant stream of dense, mephitic smoke forming large grotesque shapes in the sky before dissipating into nothingness. The band played. The cymbals crashed. The smoke rose.

Henry had heard rumors of this place for the past two years, but now it was a terrifying reality. He had arrived at the killing factory. This was surely his last stop. Here were the gas chambers. Here were the crematoriums. Here were the barracks packed with emaciated souls surviving on nothing but false hope and unanswered prayers to a

God that didn't seem to be listening. His heart sank with fear, terror, and resignation.

"We are finished," Henry whispered acquiescently to his cousin.

"Not so sure, Henry; not so sure," Leon confidently replied as he pointed to a line of prisoners. "You see how they're lining us up?" he asked. "There's going to be a selection. It's not over yet. C'mon, stand tall. Look strong."

Among the chaos and confusion, a German officer could be heard over the loudspeaker. "Achtung. Achtung!" ("Attention. Attention!") "You have arrived at Auschwitz-Birkenau Konzentrationslager. You will remain in your line and wait for our Chief Medical Officer, Dr. Mengele, to determine if you are fit for work."

As thousands of men, women, and children were spilling out of the freight cars and ordered into neat orderly rows, a man in a German uniform followed by six or seven other officers was walking up and down each row, slowly passing each person as they stood shoulder to shoulder.

"Do you see that man, Hennek?" Leon asked. "The rumor is true. That's Josef Mengele." Leon's voice faded as he finished his sentence, wishing it weren't so. "With the wave of his hand, Hennek, he is deciding, right now, who will live and who will die."

Henry saw Mengele in the distance in full SS uniform. He was surprised at how young and handsome he looked.

There seemed to be an air of delight in his stride and facial features. He was wearing a gray jacket with a black collar donning the markings of Hauptsturmfuhrer (Captain). He was heavily decorated with badges and patches and a large Iron Cross hung below his left chest pocket. His jacket was buttoned all the way to the top, and his slacks were tucked into his tall, black, shiny boots. As he walked down the rows of pitiable people, he effortlessly waved his hand to the right or left. He looked at each person for a moment and waved: To the right…to the left…to the left. He was getting closer to where Henry and Leon were standing. Right…left…left. His finger waved as he passed each person, sealing their destiny as they were quickly moved by armed guards onto open trucks that drove them into the camp. "But what does it mean?" Henry asked Leon. The reply was: "One line, you live. The other…" Leon shook his head.

Henry looked around and saw some loose dirt on the ground. "I'm too short," he thought to himself. "I need to put some of this dirt in my shoes." He quickly bent down and packed some dirt in each of his shoes, making himself a couple of inches taller. Right…right… left. Mengele was quickly approaching. He walked up to Leon. Henry's heart was racing. Mengele's finger moved right. Leon stepped away. Mengele now looked Henry in the face. As Henry looked straight into Mengele's eyes, there was no way he could have known that he was staring straight into the embodiment of Nazi ideology. Henry, a mere boy, barely 16 years old, cut off from the world for the past few years—no newspaper, no radio, no information from the outside world other than rumor and hearsay—could not have possibly understood the thought-process that was going on inside Mengele's brain behind those two eyes.

Mengele was firmly convinced that he was part of the superior Aryan race, and that he was uniquely responsible for shaping the destiny of mankind by ridding the Earth of the inferior Jews—a task which the world would thank him for in a few short years. According to Mengele, the Jew may be intelligent, but he is morally, spiritually, artistically, and physically inferior to all other races. In his view, the Jew's intelligence enabled him to thrive and succeed in the world, but only by undermining and perverting the civilization of other races. Jews were considered by him to be Untermenschen (subhuman). They were like a plague of rats that needed extermination, and he was proud to be the man who was making that happen with each wave of his superior hand each glorious moment of every day.

When Henry looked into the eyes of this young German officer, this doctor, this Angel of Death, all he could think was: "Please, God, make him wave his finger to the right." Mengele looked Henry over for a brief moment. "What if he notices the dirt in my shoes?"

Henry nervously thought to himself while holding his breath. Mengele waved him to the right. He was spared. Henry slowly exhaled. "The dirt in the shoes worked," he excitedly thought to himself. "An angel must have been watching over me and put that idea in my head." He turned and caught up to Leon, who patted him on the back. "Don't ever give up, my boy. Don't ever give up!" Leon assured him.

They were hurried off to another area where Henry noticed a row of machines flanked by German soldiers. Each prisoner was rolling up his left sleeve and placing his arm into the machine. They were receiving a tattooed number on their arm. Henry noticed that everyone was placing their arm in the machine with their forearm turned downward. When it was his turn, for a moment he hesitated and thought to himself: "If I put my arm in face down, then the tattoo will be on the top of my arm. I don't want that." He put his arm in face up. The German officer set the number into the machine and it started up. It was loud and hurt like hell. Henry made a small grimace and it was over. No one seemed to notice. He then realized that he could've been shot for what he had just done, but he didn't care. He was then moved to another area and given a tiny bowl of soup and a small piece of bread. He and Leon, along with hundreds of other men in striped uniforms, were then loaded back into another freight car.

As Henry waited for the car to fill up to capacity, he couldn't help but notice the desperate plight of the thousands of people outside. "Is this what happened to my mother and father?" he thought. "Did they arrive here with my little brothers Avram and Chaim and my older sisters Celina and Sala holding their suitcases and bundles in their hands? Were they unloaded and lined up for Mengele to decide their destiny? Did they survive the train ride? How scared Avram and Chaim must have been, my mother holding their little hands as they marched from one line to the next. Were they one of the screaming children on that truck a little while ago?" He continued to wonder if his sisters were among those shaven-headed, skeleton-like women whom he saw being loaded onto a truck and taken inside the camp. He felt that this might have been where they perished, and he wondered if those grotesque shapes of smoke coming from those stacks were the silhouetted remains of his family drifting into oblivion, forever forgotten. Surely Mengele would have chosen his father to live. Or was he considered too old at age 56 to be useful anymore and gestured to the left? "Good god!" Henry cried out. "How can they be doing this? Why? What did we do?"

The train car was packed again to the point where not another soul could fit inside. As the door began to roll closed, Henry looked around inside the car and saw nothing but desperate faces full of fear, anger, disbelief, and resignation. A small trickle of light spilled through the tiny window. Henry looked down at his still bleeding and swollen tattoo. He was no longer a human being with a name. Now he was merely another number in the Nazi machinery of death—149824.

Henry's mother Ida, circa 1939. Only existing photo.

Henry's father Zygmund, circa 1939. Only existing photo.

Henry's oldest sister Sala with her husband Moishe, circa 1939.
One of two existing photos.

Henry's older sister Celina, circa 1939.
Only existing photo.

Henry shortly after liberation. 1945.

Henry in Krakow, 1945, with his first nephew Ygnaz.

Henry meets his sister-in-law Basha and his first nephew Ygnaz
in Krakow, 1945.

Henry shortly before traveling to America. 1947.

Henry in Munich with Italian soldier, 1945.

Henry having fun in Munich, 1947.

GOOD FOR SINGLE JOURNEY TO USA ONLY

CERTIFICATE OF IDENTITY IN LIEU OF PASSPORT

AMERICAN CONSULATE GENERAL, MUNICH GERMANY

17899

Date   June 4th 1947

1. This is to certify that   Hennek KOPERWAS   , born at
                                   (name in full)

Germany   Dortmund   Westfalia   on   1st
(country)   (town)   (District)   (day)

(age) 1926   male   single
(month) (year)   (sex)   (marital status)

xxx
(place and maiden name of wife)   intends to immigrate to

USA

2. He (she) will be accompanied by   Nobody

(Here list all family members by name,
birthplace and date, together with citizen-
ship of each)

3. His (her) occupation is   Lock smith

4. DESCRIPTION

Height   ft.   5   in.

Hair brown Eyes blue

Distinguishing marks or features:

Number, 149824, from cons. camp

Dachau on left forearm

5. He (she) solemnly declares that he has never committed nor has he been convicted of any crime except as follows

xxx

6. He is unable to produce birth certificate, marriage license, divorce papers and/or police record for the following
reason(s)   xxx

I hereby certify that the above are true facts, proper photograph and description of Myself.

Subscribed and sworn to before me this 4th   day of   June 1947

Hennek Koperwas   _Thomas A. Moore_
(Signature of applicant)   (Signature of consul)

Hennek KOPERWAS   Fee No 24   9394
$ 2.- equal to 20.-   JUN 20 1947
Service No.   (Date)

454-7/48 - Printed by Ludwig Starr, München 29, Liebherrstr. 3

Henry's Certificate of Identity in Lieu of Passport obtained in Munich,
June 4, 1947 shortly before his trip to America.

UNRRA AREA TEAM 1026
Emigrant Staging Area Bremen

Name: Koperwas, Henek
Date of small pox Vaccination   4 Juli 1947
Date of control examination   7. Juli 1947
Type of Reaction   a/ Reaction of immunity
                    b/ Accelerated Reaction
                    c/ Typical primary vaccine.

(Cross out reactions not applicable).

Signature of doctor:
Official position: U.N.R.R. ed. Officer
DR. GUILLERMO LOPEZ DE SILVA
IDENTIFICATION No 8
U.N.R.R.A. MEDICAL OFFICER

Henry's Immunization Record obtained at the Medical Center at UNRRA
(United Nations Relief and Rehabilitation Administration), Bremen,
Germany, just one day before his journey to America.

EMBARKATION CARD
Einschiffungskarte

S/S

Sailing-Date:

Accommodation   C 40 - 31
Schiffsplatz

Mr.
Mrs.   KOPERWAS, Henek
Miss

Nr. 21 A 850

Henry's Embarkation Card for the SS Marine Marlin bound for America.

Henry's passenger ticket to America dated July 8, 1947.

Chapter 6

Eating With Swine

WHEN YOU'RE HUNGRY ALL THE TIME THERE'S NOT MUCH ELSE you think about. Family members, friends, the past and future, are all subordinated to the task at hand: satisfying that inexorable gnawing hunger that consumes your attention. For Henry, it began as soon as he woke up till the time he went to sleep. It had been over two years since he was separated from his family members, yet he didn't cry anymore. In fact, he almost never thought about them, at least not consciously. Instead, his waking moments were filled with nothing but thoughts of survival: how to get enough food to stay alive. A bowl of watery soup once a day was not enough to sustain a human being. Henry had to steal food from the German soldiers or from the potato fields nearby. Fortunately he knew someone who was giving out the daily rations of soup and was making sure his scoop came from the bottom of the pot where some of the vegetables were lying. That helped a great deal but it wasn't enough.

If he was lucky he could make it one more day. But for what? When you were exhausted and of no more use to the Nazis, they would dispose of you like a broken part in a machine. Still, deep in his subconscious Henry had hope: an irrational belief that somehow things would be different tomorrow. Somehow—God knows how, but somehow—things would be better. After all, just a few years ago things were drastically different for him when he was living with his family in Radom. Compared to his situation at present, life then was great, even though they were living in squalor in the ghetto. Now, just a few years later, everything was different. Deep down inside himself, he believed that things could change quickly again for the better. As hard as it was to believe, he felt that the Germans could be stopped and he would be set free—free to find his family and to live his life as he chose. Remarkably, hope was still alive in him.

When he arrived at the labor camp in Vaihingen he was given a new uniform. He took off his old lice-ridden one that he had been wearing for almost two years. He knew that the new uniform was most likely worn by someone else who had died in it, but he didn't care. It was clean. He was allowed to work with his older cousin Leon in his tailor shop. The Germans needed a small group of tailors to mend their uniforms. Henry was one of ten people who had the privilege of working indoors, escaping the brutal cold of the outside. He knew nothing about tailoring when he started working there, but under Leon's tutelage he caught on quickly. Another older cousin of his, Saul, worked as a cobbler and was able to get him a decent pair of German army shoes as well. To

Henry these were the most beautiful shoes he had ever seen. He felt privileged to have them and he guarded them with his life.

In order to survive on the tiny rations of food he was given, it would be necessary to obtain additional food somehow. Sometimes Henry or his friends Walter and Felix had to work in the airfield nearby in Unterriexingen, and there was a field of potatoes adjacent to it. They took turns sneaking the potatoes into the camp by rolling them under the fence when the German guards were not watching. Walter knew a little bit about electricity. At night when everyone was asleep, Henry, Walter, and Felix would cook their still-frozen potatoes by disconnecting the wires from the single light bulb in their barracks and using the electrical current to heat up water in a metal bowl. They had to be extra cautious not to get caught by the German soldiers or by the Jewish Kapos (trustee inmates) who patrolled the barracks at night keeping watch over several thousand men. Henry particularly hated these Kapos. He couldn't understand how someone could turn on their fellow Jews in order to obtain special privileges from the Germans.

*   *   *   *   *

One day after several months of working with his cousin Leon, Henry noticed that his friend Walter didn't have any shoes. Someone had stolen them during the night while he was sleeping. He was working outside in the bitter cold with nothing but cement paper wrapped around his feet. Feeling sorry for his friend, Henry gave him his cherished shoes thinking that he would get another pair from his cousin Saul. It was early in the morning, just before their daily line up.

A little while later Henry stood outside along with three thousand other men. The Obersturmbannfuhrer of the camp was named Hecker. When he saw Henry standing barefoot in the freezing cold he stopped in front of him.

"Where are your shoes?" Hecker asked.

"Someone stole them while I was sleeping," Henry quickly replied, thinking that he would then be given another pair.

"Is that so?" Hecker replied in a punitive tone. "Well then, let us take a walk up and down these rows of men and you can tell me which one of them is wearing your shoes."

Henry's heart sank into the pit of his gut. "I can't possibly reveal who has my shoes," he thought to himself while slowly walking from person to person, not knowing how to get out his conundrum. "Hecker will surely kill the man who I point out to discourage anyone from doing the same thing. He is going to set an example in front of everyone else."

Henry remembered, in a sudden flash of horror, the time when he was marching back from the airfield after a long day of exhausting labor along with several hundred other men. Standing next to him was a boy his age, around 15 or so. He was sickly-looking and had pimples on his face. As the group approached the entrance gate, something about this boy caught the attention of Obersturmbannfuhrer Hecker who suddenly stopped them. "Halt," he yelled, with an almost gleeful tone. Evidently, he noticed a slight bulge in this poor lad's uniform. "Empty your pocket, you filthy Jew," he demanded. The boy looked around for a way out. Henry remembered the desperation on his face that quickly turned to resignation once he realized that he was doomed. The officer became impatient and reached into his pocket, pulling out a single potato. He threw it on the ground with such force that it exploded into pieces. Without saying a word, he reached for his sidearm. He unsnapped the leather case, drew his Luger, and without a moment's hesitation he shot the boy in the side of the head. Everyone was startled. His head exploded just like the potato had. Pieces of his brain splattered about, some of it hitting Henry in the face. "Now, all of you clean up this mess and get this schweinehund (pig-dog) out of my sight," the furious Hecker commanded. Henry remembered being both horrified and disgusted as he picked pieces of human flesh off the barbed wire fence.

"I'm going to wind up just like that kid," Henry thought. After walking up and down a few rows of men he saw Walter standing in line wearing his shoes. Walter could see the anguish in Henry's eyes as he approached. They briefly made eye contact when Henry stopped. He turned toward Hecker with a look of desperation.

"I'm sorry," he began. "It's impossible for me to tell who has my shoes. They all look the same. I can't be certain." He stood motionless as everyone looked on.

"Then you will have to go without shoes," Hecker replied. "And you will no longer work here as a tailor. We need more men at the airfield in Unterriexingen. You will work there from now on."

Hearing this Leon approached Hecker. "But sir," he began in a pleading voice, trying to save his little cousin from hard labor. "He is one of my best tailors. I need him to be able to do my work." Without hesitation Hecker swung his arm toward Leon striking him across the face with the back of his hand. Leon fell violently backwards hitting the hard ground. Hecker came over to him and began shouting while pointing his finger, "If you don't get up and get out of my sight I will shoot you on the spot!" Leon quickly pulled himself up from the ground and got back in line. The Obersturmbannfuhrer ordered Henry to line up with a group of other men who would be sent to work in the nearby airfield.

Later that day at Unterriexingen Henry was put to work at the airfield patching holes in the runway. The Americans and the Soviets were continually bombing, so the work never ended. The winter cold was relentless. Luckily, Leon gave Henry an old discarded German uniform to wear under his striped prison clothes. This kept him relatively warm. He had to be sure that none of it showed through his striped uniform or the Nazis would certainly kill him for the transgression. It was a risk he was willing to take considering the extreme cold. He now had no shoes. As his friend Walter had previously done, he wore paper from the cement bags around his feet to try to keep them warm. As he was mixing concrete his feet became numb. After standing still for some time he tried to move his feet but couldn't. They were frozen to the ground. The water he was using to mix the cement had frozen under his feet. Noticing this, the others helped him to break loose with the use of their tools. Actually, Henry was not concentrating on his work at hand. He was eyeing a farmhouse across from the airfield and was thinking about nothing but food— how to satisfy his perpetual hunger.

There were several pigs and some chickens just a few hundred yards away. Surely he could find something to eat there, he thought, and he no longer even cared if the Germans shot him. He was so hungry that he didn't even notice that his feet had frozen to the ground a little while ago. He was determined to make a run for it. While contemplating risking his life for animal feed, a group of American bomber planes flew overhead. When Henry and his small group of companions saw the planes, they began waving their arms up at the sky cheering the bombers on. They all wished the Americans would obliterate their camp and kill every last Nazi there, and they didn't care if they themselves died in the process. Their ordeal would be over and the Germans would be stopped. Then they saw the bombs rain down from the sky.

As everyone ran for cover and the German guards were distracted, Henry made his move. He ran across the field attached to the airstrip and over to where the animals were being kept. As he got closer he noticed a feeding trough for the pigs with fresh, still-warm feed inside. He chased the pigs away and dove face-first into their food. He felt as though he was in heaven and ate until he couldn't eat anymore. As his hunger became satisfied he started to feel somewhat embarrassed by his rapacious behavior. "Look at me," he thought to himself. "I'm worse than these pigs. How did this happen to me? I'm like an animal." He paused in remorse.

"Hey you, what are you doing?" an angry voice called out in German. Henry looked up and saw a farmer standing over him.

"I'm sorry," Henry replied in German as he stood up. "I was hungry and couldn't help myself."

"You need to leave here at once and go back where you belong," the farmer demanded as he pointed to the airfield nearby.

"Please, sir," Henry pleaded, "I can't go back there. Please help me. Take me in. I will work for you. You can say I am your son. No one will know."

"No one will know? Look at you. You are a Jew. Your head is shaved and you have that uniform on."

"I can wear a hat until my hair grows back. I'm sure you have just one pair of trousers and a shirt I can wear," Henry pleaded.

"No. It is not possible. I have a wife and a family. If the Nazis find out, they will kill us all. You must go now," he insisted, as he grabbed Henry by the arm and started walking him out of the barn.

What Henry did not know was that the people of Germany saw the Jew as an outsider, as something *other*. Being Jewish was not just a religion; it was not a matter of a chosen faith. There was no choice involved. You were born a Jew. It was your race. Throughout modern history the view of many in Christendom was that the Jews rejected the true messiah and conspired to kill him. They worshipped in a different way and in a different language to a different God. They wore different clothes and ate different food. They kept to themselves in their shtetlekh (small towns). They spoke their own language, Yiddish. They even had their own laws and councils to administer and adjudicate those laws. They never fully assimilated into society. Their loyalty to their respective nations was always in question. Were they Germans or Jews? They were a people with no homeland, a people of the diaspora. A people with a hyphenated identity. Historically, Jews were treated as second-class citizens wherever they lived in Europe. No one could figure out what to do with them. In a word, they were a problem.

Over time many solutions to this problem came and went, from every new law to every new round of confiscation, expulsion, and exile. Then Hitler and the Nazi Party came to power in the 1930s. According to Hitler, Germany (then the Weimar Republic) had been plagued by the problem of the Jew for far too long. It was the itinerant Jew, with no permanent place in Europe, who was responsible for starting World War I. It was the Jew who was responsible for giving Germany a bad deal at the treaty of Versailles which led to the collapse of the German economy. The Jews controlled the politicians, the banks, and the financial institutions—this is how the thinking went. They were responsible for Jewish Marxism, the enemy of German National Socialism and part of the Zionist plot to take over the world. Jews were not true Germans, not Aryans. They were a lesser race and had become a bigger problem than ever before. If they weren't stopped it would be too late, and the solution was not to just drive them out of Europe because eventually they would come back. They had to be exterminated for good. That is the only solution that is permanent and once-and-for-all. In other words, it is the "Final Solution."

Having been separated from his home and education at a young age, Henry was unschooled in world affairs. He was unaware of the politics and ideology that surrounded him and led to the current war in Europe and to his enslavement and struggle. He didn't know that for the past several centuries in almost every country in Europe at one time or another, there were special laws on the books specifically limiting the rights of Jews: where they had to live, who they could and could not marry, what professions they were barred from engaging in, what kind of clothes or special markings they had to wear, how much special poll tax they had to pay to their respective governments, and where they could worship or build their synagogues. Sometimes Jewish families had their sons taken by the government to be raised as "good Christians" or to be conscripted into the army to fight their wars. But Henry was unaware of all this. Just a short time ago, without warning, he and his family were driven from their home by the Nazis, all of their property and personal belongings were seized, and they were forced to live in a deplorable ghetto. Then he was ripped away from all that he had, which was his family, and he has been struggling alone to stay alive ever since. Why he and all other Jews were being victimized was beyond his understanding. He only knew that this was his reality.

The farmer led Henry to the road and told him to never come back. Henry was filled with anger and disbelief. He hated this man for not helping him. "Why would he not take me in?" he thought. "He's just like all the other Germans—a Jew-hater." Henry felt utterly alone and that the entire world was conspiring against him. "Where can I go?" he thought to himself. "No one will take me in. I can't hide forever." He knew that he had no choice but to go back. If he didn't get back soon, he would be noticed missing and the guards would come looking for him, and when they found him they would most definitely shoot him. He wished that he had stuffed his pockets with the pig feed so that he could eat some more of it again later, but remembering what happened to the pimple-faced boy with the potato, he knew that it was probably better that he hadn't. With the farmer watching him he ran back toward the airstrip and hid in some nearby bushes waiting for the right moment to slip back through the fence unseen by the guards.

Once again Henry heard planes in the sky. He looked up and saw several American fighter planes heading toward the airstrip. They began firing their machine guns at the German soldiers. This was his chance to get back unnoticed. He ran toward the airstrip shouting: "Kill them all! Die, you rotten sons-of-bitches!" After a short distance he crept under the fence in the spot where he had escaped earlier. As he got up and ran back toward his group of workers, the fighter planes circled back around. They came in again with their guns riddling the ground with bullets. He could hear the bullets whizzing past his head. He dove to the ground and took cover.

Suddenly he felt a terrible burning sensation in his foot. He looked up and saw someone from his group fall to the ground with a large bloody hole in his chest. He had been hit in the heart. The bullet kept going and came out of this fellow's back, tore through a steel wheelbarrow, and grazed Henry's foot. "I'm hit," he shouted, while screaming from the pain. He started crying and thought he was going to die. The pain was unbearable. His friend Abe came over to comfort him and looked at the wound. "You're not going to die, Henry," he reassured him. "Luckily it's just a surface wound." Abe tore a piece of cloth from Henry's uniform and wrapped it around the wound to stop the bleeding. He then went over to check on the other man who was hit. He was dead. Suddenly the planes were gone and the shooting stopped. Before the German soldiers came out to examine the damage to the airfield, Henry and Abe headed back to the camp to find the doctor, who was a Jew as well. While the doctor was dressing Henry's wound, he told him that if he reported his injury to the Nazis, they would certainly kill him. "You'll have to go back to work," he reluctantly informed Henry. Even though the pain was unbearable, it didn't overpower Henry's will to live. He stood up and practiced walking without a limp so that the Germans wouldn't notice that he was injured.

As he walked back to the airstrip with Abe he noticed that for the first time since he could remember, he wasn't thinking about eating. His stomach was not calling out for food. Instead he had to deal with excruciating pain in his foot. It was a worthwhile trade-off for now. He wiped the tears from his eyes and concentrated on walking without favoring his injured foot. After a short time they got back to the airstrip. Although Henry's foot was throbbing, he picked up a shovel and began filling the newly-formed craters from the recent bombing. He looked over to the pigs, who were happily gorging themselves. As he reluctantly shoveled gravel into a pothole, he thought to himself: "They don't know how good they have it!" He wished he could trade places with them.

Chapter 7

Buried Treasure

THE COMMANDANT OF KL KOCHENDORF ADDRESSED Henry and the rest of the newly-arrived group of men with a stern voice. "You will all be working in these salt mines," he began. "You will be given special food that is slightly greasy in order to absorb the salt that you will be breathing while inside the mines. You will be given a ration of water as well. If you drink more than is given to you, you will wind up like those people," he warned while pointing to a pile of corpses. Seeing this Henry was shocked. "Those are your people," he continued. "They didn't follow my orders. Do not make the same mistake," he concluded and walked away. Henry looked around and saw people working in conditions that he had never witnessed before. Most of the men were extremely malnourished. They looked like living skeletons. He wondered how they were able to stand and move about. "This is a death camp," he thought to himself. "The Nazis are going to work me until I fall over and die." As he was wondering how he would survive in the living hell that was displayed before him, a Ukrainian Kapo shouted out for everyone to line up. All the men slowly fell in line.

The Kapo began selecting men for various tasks within the salt mines. Henry noticed that besides the Jewish prisoners there were also POWs from various neighboring countries. He would be working side by side with them. He was given a tool for digging and led into the salt mine. The entrance to the mine was a three-story brick building with a metal scaffolding superstructure attached to it. The structure stood about 75 feet tall and had large pulleys at the top with thick steel cables wrapped around them that would lower and raise an elevator deep into the mine shaft. Several rows of railroad tracks ran up to the entrance that were used to bring the excavated salt out and away from the mine, as well as to bring trainloads of various items to be stored in the mines.

German scientists had determined that using salt mines to store various plundered items that were confiscated from Jews or taken from countries they had occupied was an ideal way of preserving those items. The constant temperature of about 50 degrees Fahrenheit and the stable humidity of roughly 60-65 percent would almost guarantee that deposited works of art would not be damaged by any sudden changes of heat or moisture. The Kochendorf salt mine sat about 35 feet above the water level so there was no danger of water seeping into the mine. The Nazis had been bringing their most cherished items here for months: paintings, sculptures, statues, and other rare items, and they needed a constant supply of slave labor to expand their enterprise by digging new tunnels.

Henry and his group were led by the Kapo down into the mine shaft. They walked through a long narrow tunnel about 20 feet wide and 10 feet high that had been carved directly into solid salt-rock and came to an area where the tunnel had ended. Men were busily chipping away at a solid wall while German soldiers stood by at watch. Henry's job was to break off large pieces of rock and load them into a steel mining car that was hauled off by other workers. It was extremely loud and dusty. He wore no mask or any kind of protective gear and hadn't eaten any food all day. He started working while planning on how he could get his hands on some extra food rations.

After several hours of exhausting work Henry noticed two German soldiers taking their lunch break. They sat off to the side and opened their knapsacks which contained their food. Henry kept an eye on them while he kept working. When the soldiers were done they left their knapsacks off to the side and went back to guarding the workers. Looking around to make sure no other guards were watching him, Henry cautiously walked over and grabbed one of the knapsacks. He took it back to where he was working and buried it under some salt rocks that had piled up on the tunnel floor. He kept on working while contemplating what might be inside. The other men were too busy with their own tasks to notice what he was up to.

A few minutes later when the guards were out of sight, he pulled the bag out from the rubble and carried it off to an area where he couldn't be seen. Opening the knapsack, he pulled out a can of sardines and some bread. He was thrilled. He hid them both and then went back to where the soldiers ate their lunch and put the knapsack back where he found it. He then went back to work. The German soldiers came back around to check on the workers. When they left again he nonchalantly walked over to his buried treasure and quickly devoured the can of sardines and bread and then went back to his work. As he started breaking away chunks of rock-salt, he smiled knowing that he now had a way of staying alive as long as he didn't get caught.

*　　　*　　　*　　　*　　　*

Several months had gone by. It was the middle of the night. Henry and his group were awakened by the Ukrainian Kapo. He was taking count to see if anyone had escaped. He knew that if anyone went missing, the German officers in charge of the camp would blame him for it. He had to be vigilant, and he was. Eventually this became a nightly routine. Henry couldn't remember ever getting a full night's rest without being harassed by this man. As the Kapo walked through the barracks holding a baton, he noticed a man still lying in his bed. He struck him across the chest swiftly with his baton, making a loud sound upon impact that made everyone cringe. The man jumped out of bed in fear and pain while managing to get himself in line without falling over. The Kapo then checked around and under each bed to see if there was any stolen food to confiscate. On this night he found nothing. He then began addressing the men while tapping his baton into the open palm of his hand. "All of you need to line up outside at once," he commanded. "You are being moved to Dachau." He then turned around and started walking toward the door. Another prisoner started to ask a question, but before he could get three words out the Kapo beat him across his shoulder with his baton. The man fell to the ground in pain and the Kapo walked out. Henry looked around and could see the hate in all the other men's eyes for this man. If they had the chance they would rip him to pieces with their bare hands. "For now he is in charge, but his luck may change some day," Henry thought to himself. He and his group of men then went outside to line up for their journey to Dachau.

The trip would be a long one. The Germans were short on trucks that could be used for transportation of prisoners so the trek would have to be done on foot. Henry had no idea how long he would be walking or exactly where Dachau was, or what would happen to him once he arrived there. The one thing he knew for sure was that he was happy to be leaving the salt mines. He didn't know how much longer he could survive in that unbearable place. He was relieved that he would no longer be doing hard labor for twelve hours a day in horrific conditions.

Hundreds of men were lined up. They walked four abreast. Armed German soldiers flanked each side of the line. Every few hours another man would collapse from exhaustion and malnutrition. When someone fell to the ground the marching men walked around or over them. Henry had no idea what became of them. He just kept moving without looking back.

Henry walked for several hours through the night. The sun began to rise revealing a small town in the distance. The early morning fog was rising as smoke drifted from the chimneys of quaint buildings, carrying the aromas of breakfast. Henry felt his hunger increase. His stomach felt like a hollow cave. As he and his group passed through the center of town a crowd of local people gathered on either side of the street. They temporarily paused from their early morning routine to look on as though these men were part of a macabre parade. Men, women, and small children yelled insulting epithets as Henry's group slowly marched past, forming a river of decrepit striped uniforms animated by ghosts of their former selves. Henry saw one young boy standing with his mother. As Henry passed, the boy threw a small stone and yelled, "Verflucht Jude!" ("Accursed Jew!") He then ran alongside the marching men, continually taunting them while throwing stones.

Amidst the humiliation, fatigue, and hunger, Henry saw an apple core lying in the road several feet ahead of him. It was slightly rotten but still had some fruit on it. Without hesitation he leaned over to pick it up, but before his hand could reach it he felt a stinging sensation in his back between his shoulder blades. He screamed and threw both his arms into the air as he quickly straightened up to see what had happened. A German soldier who was walking beside him pulled back his bayonet attached to the end of his rifle while shouting, "Schweinehund, keep moving!" Henry thought he was going to die. The pain was unbearable. "That filthy son of a bitch stabbed me," Henry thought to himself while he kept walking. "What does it matter to him if I pick up a scrap of food?" He tried desperately to hold back his anger. He looked to his side, and to his surprise he saw his older cousin Leon making his way over. Henry hadn't seen Leon since leaving Unterriexingen many months ago. Now happenstance had brought them together once again.

Leon walked alongside Henry and draped his arm around his shoulder, pressing the back of his uniform firmly into his wound. Henry grimaced. "You're going to live, Hennek," Leon assured him. "The bayonet didn't go too deep. You're lucky. Thank God." Hearing this, Henry actually felt disappointed. He was exhausted and hungry, and death seemed like the only relief from the misery he felt, both physically and mentally. Leon explained to Henry that he heard rumors that the Germans were bringing them to Dachau to be traded to the British or to the Americans in exchange for captured German soldiers. Hearing this news Henry's eyes lit up with hope. The thought of his ordeal coming to an end gave him the strength to live and to keep walking. He told Leon how happy he was to see him again. In spite of his extreme pain, he held his head up and pressed forward with a renewed stride.

The sun continued its journey upward, illuminating the seemingly endless road ahead. Henry saw a small bird flying past him slightly overhead, a rotten apple core dangling from its beak. He watched it with envy as it disappeared into the trees.

Chapter 8

Born Again

FOR THE FIRST TIME SINCE HE COULD REMEMBER, HENRY was happy and hopeful. When he first arrived at Dachau he immediately noticed how easy the prisoners had it. "These people look like they get enough food to actually stay alive," he pleasantly thought to himself. "Maybe those rumors about being traded for German prisoners are true after all." The conditions Henry was used to were a thousand times worse than what he now saw. He was led to his barrack along with several dozen other Jewish prisoners wearing striped uniforms. They walked down a narrow road with long single-story buildings on either side. He saw Americans, Canadians, Russians, and Frenchmen all busy hanging their clothes out to dry, cleaning, working on small tasks, and most surprisingly, lounging about. "There's no forced labor?" he wondered to himself. "Wow, this is like a convalescent home."

A German officer brought Henry and his group to a building where they were instructed to take off their clothes and shower. They were given fresh uniforms. "You are now political prisoners of the German Army," he announced. "The Red Cross is here doing an inspection. You will not talk to them. If you are heard speaking with them you will be dealt with harshly. "Verstehen?" ("Do you understand?") The officer then left the building. Henry understood. He would not be telling the Red Cross how he just came from the salt mines in Kochendorf and witnessed hundreds of men expire from exhaustion and malnutrition. He would be silent about how he had to steal food from the knapsacks of German soldiers when their backs were turned, risking his life so that he wouldn't starve to death while he did back-breaking slave labor for twelve hours a day. He would not say a word about the long march to Dachau, with nothing to eat for days, and how he watched men drop dead by the dozens as he walked beside them. He would say nothing about how he reached down to pick up a rotten apple core he saw lying on the road, only to be stabbed in the back by a bayonet on the end of German officer's rifle. No, he was not going to ruin his chances of being traded for German soldiers and gaining his freedom. There would be plenty of time to speak later if he was lucky enough to live until then.

Henry couldn't believe that he had his own cot to sleep on and that he didn't have to share it with three or four other men. As the men began settling into their new surroundings they began talking about rumors they each heard of what was going to happen to them.

"The Germans are short of supplies and trucks," one man voiced aloud. "That is why they are trading us."

"No, no," retorted another. "We're being traded for German prisoners; that's why the Red Cross is here."

"Didn't you see all those men outside?" a third man questioned. "Why would they trade us? Look at us. There are so many other men who are strong and fit. It doesn't make sense."

"That's exactly it," replied another. "They want to trade off the weaker prisoners first."

Henry was confused and didn't know what to believe. One thing was certain, though: things were much better where he was now than anywhere he had been in the past several years. Several nurses from the Red Cross entered Henry's barrack to speak to him and his group. The nurses were shocked to see how emaciated they were. They brought in packages of food but warned everyone to be very careful not to eat too much. They had seen many people die from eating rich foods after being malnourished for so many years. Henry gladly accepted the food and was careful to only eat very small portions, gradually allowing his body to adjust to the new food.

While sitting on his bed savoring his first decent meal in recent memory, Henry noticed a man standing around looking nervous. At first Henry didn't recognize him because he was not wearing his usual uniform from the camp at Kochendorf. Henry then realized that this was the Ukrainian Kapo who would wake everyone up in the middle of the night and harass and torment his fellow prisoners. He gave everyone a hard time and made life miserable for them. A few other men recognized him as well, and one large Russian guy spoke up so that everyone could hear. "Well, look who they put in here with us," he said sarcastically. "Now you're just one of us," he continued in a menacing tone while glancing around the room.

The Kapo looked around nervously, knowing that he was in for it. Before he had a chance to reply, several men attacked him. Six or seven men pounced on him, kicking and punching. One man tore a leg off his bed and began beating the ex-Kapo across the back. He broke loose and began to run, but there was nowhere to go. Badly beaten and looking around in confusion he realized that he was cornered. The men ran toward him again. In a desperate panic he jumped through a closed window that was behind him. Glass shattered as he fell to the ground, and the other men jumped through the broken window after him. Henry ran over to the window and looked down as the men stood over their victim repeatedly kicking him and beating him until he stopped moving. When they walked away, all that Henry could make out was a bloody pile of what was once a person. "You son of a bitch, you had it coming to you," Henry thought to himself as he walked over to his bunk bed feeling that justice had been served. He began eating his food. Slowly.

After a few months of what Henry would call luxury living, a train pulled into Dachau. Henry and several thousand other Jewish men were told that they were being taken to Austria to be traded for German prisoners. Everyone was thrilled. Henry grabbed his few belongings: a change of clothes, his bowl and spoon, a blanket. He walked outside with a feeling of joy and relief. "I can't believe this is happening," he thought to himself. He was loaded into a long train that had so many cars that he couldn't see to the end of it. Unlike his horrendous journey to Auschwitz when he was crammed into a car with over two hundred people, the car he was loaded into only held about thirty-five to fifty other people. There were armed German soldiers on the outside of each car standing on small platforms with rifles. The cars were mostly open at the top. Henry was not in the dark, dank, miserable conditions of just a few months ago. As they travelled into the Swiss Alps on that wintery day sometime at the end of April, Henry stared at the stunning landscape outside. As the train climbed the mountains he noticed snow-covered trees, majestic mountains, and sweeping valleys. "I can't believe this could all be over," Henry thought. For the first time since he could remember, he started wondering about the fate of the rest of his family. He was all alone now and the last time he saw anyone from his immediate family was several years ago, though he couldn't remember exactly when. Time had no meaning to him anymore; a day, a month, a year—it was hard to tell just how much time had passed.

As the train continued deep into the Swiss Alps, day gave way to darkness. The train kept on and Henry fell asleep. When he awoke it was light again, and once again the train pushed forward all day long. Henry had no food or water and he was cold. It was just starting to get dark when he heard aircraft overhead. He looked up and caught a glimpse of an American bomber plane releasing its payload. As the cluster of bombs sailed to the ground, Henry covered his head with both his arms while sitting on the train floor, his back pressed against the wall and his knees raised to his chest as he braced for the pending impact. The bombs exploded just a few hundred yards away, sending debris flying in all directions. The train came to a screeching halt as everyone flew forward in the car tumbling over one another. The tracks were badly damaged and the train could go no further.

Many German guards jumped off the train and ran to the front to see what had happened. They began instructing everyone to get out of their cars. "Everyone get down. Out, out!" they started screaming. The soldiers instructed everyone to assemble on a small plateau a short distance from where the train had stopped. As Henry was getting down from his car he saw a civilian woman riding a bicycle on a small, partially snow-covered road that ran adjacent to the train tracks. She was waving her hand at the SS officer, trying to get his attention. She seemed very excited. "Please listen," she screamed in German. "The Americans are close by. Now you have the chance to escape and save yourselves. Just leave these people here and save yourselves while you still can," she urged the officer. The officer waved back to her and assured her that everything was fine. He thanked her for her advice with a feigned smile and continued walking to the front of the train. Thousands of men gathered a few hundred feet from a forest of tall trees. Standing in snow almost up to his knees Henry could hear gunfire and explosions in the distance. He was confused and started doubting that the officer was telling the truth about being traded. "Is this son of a bitch lying to us?" he wondered. "Could it be that this monster is going to kill us all? Please, God, no!" he prayed.

Several soldiers began setting up machine guns. The woman continued pleading with the officer but he was not listening. He yelled at her and she finally rode off. "Should I run?" Henry thought to himself. "I'd be the first one they would shoot if I did that." Then Henry heard the SS officer give the command. The machine guns started firing and people all around him started falling to the ground, their bodies being riddled with bullets. Henry instinctively also dropped to the ground and dug himself deep into the snow, pushing his body close to the freezing, cold earth. Bodies were piling up all around him. People were screaming and hopelessly running for their lives.

Henry started crawling away on his belly as quickly as he could through the chaos and mayhem. He heard bullets whiz by, yet he kept moving away from the gunfire and toward the trees. He pushed bodies off himself so that he could keep moving. "I have to keep going," he screamed to himself, "because you Nazi bastards are not going to kill me. Not after everything I've been through." Determined, he kept moving, plowing his way through the snow. He was about 25 yards from the massacre when he popped his head up briefly and looked back. German soldiers were walking through the pile of bodies looking for those still alive. They stabbed this one, shot that one. "I've got to keep moving," he thought to himself.

He soon broke out of the snow and started running into the woods, his feet moving under him like the locomotive engine on the train that had brought him there. Fueled by adrenaline and fear he kept running until he was exhausted and fell to the ground. When he looked up he saw a small shack about 50 feet away which looked abandoned. He picked himself up and headed over to it and got inside. By now it was dark outside and there was no light inside. It was cold and he was exhausted. He hid in a corner, staying low and hoping that the Germans wouldn't find him. The shooting gradually stopped and a deadening silence filled the shack. Henry was shaking and breathing heavily. There was no way for him to escape if the German soldiers found him there. He rolled himself up into a fetal position. He was scared but too exhausted to run any further. Shivering, he lay there curled up in a corner until he finally fell asleep from exhaustion.

Early in the morning Henry was awakened by the sound of motorcycles. He looked outside through a small opening in the shack and saw two men on motorcycles riding toward him while talking into their radios. Just then two tanks appeared behind them and were heading straight for the shack. Henry ran to the other side of the small building and to his surprise noticed several other men doing the same. Apparently he was not the only one who got away the night before. He heard a crashing sound and turned quickly. A large gun barrel atop one of the tanks had broken through the wall. He thought he was done for, but to his surprise the tank stopped. Several soldiers with rifles came running into the building.

When Henry and the other men saw the soldiers, they raised their hands high above their heads to surrender. The soldiers stood there with their rifles pointed at them and began speaking in a language which Henry was unfamiliar with. He noticed that they were black-skinned and he was confused because he had never seen a Black man before. "Are they from Africa? Are they Russians?"

he asked himself. "What language are they speaking?" Two more Black soldiers entered the shack and began speaking in German: "We are Americans. You are safe now. We are here to help you." It was only then that Henry noticed the star on the soldiers' helmets. He and the other men spontaneously began to dance in ecstasy, jumping up and down while embracing each other and shouting: "We made it, we made it! We are free!"

Henry collapsed to the ground in tears of joy. He couldn't believe that he was alive—and free. No more Nazi sons of bitches were going to tell him what to do. No more sadistic German SS officers would force him to work without food or sleep until he felt hopeless and exhausted. He thought that maybe he was dreaming so he touched himself over and over to be sure. No, this was real; he was not dreaming. After a few moments dozens of African American soldiers arrived and comforted the men. They told them that they would be taken back to Dachau where the United States' Seventh Army's 45th Infantry Division had liberated that camp just a couple of days before. What no one knew at that time was that in just a few more days the Allied powers would defeat Hitler's army and the war would be over.

Ironically, the men that came to Henry's rescue were part of a segregated U.S. Army where Blacks and Whites could not serve their country together. On one front, they were fighting the deadly racism of the Nazi regime that

Henry was struggling to survive through. On another front, these same soldiers were fighting a different kind of racism and prejudice at home in America, where they were struggling for equal rights in a segregated U.S. military.

These Black GI's were most likely part of the 761st Tank Battalion of General Patton's Third Army. They were called the Black Panthers and their motto was "Come out fighting!" They were one of the most effective tank battalions in the war and were instrumental in taking down an evil, racist German empire. After fighting Hitler's soldiers on the beaches of Normandy and in the Ardennes at the Battle of the Bulge, they worked their way across France, through Austria and into Germany. Miraculously, a small group of them happened upon a few lucky survivors of a Nazi massacre. Only a handful of some three thousand men survived that day, and Henry was thrilled to be one of them. How ironic it was that the first Black people that Henry encountered in his life were a force of freedom and liberation, while they themselves were not truly free in their own country.

Having lost track of time, Henry asked one of the soldiers through a translator what day it was. "It's May 1st, 1945," the soldier replied. "Oh my God," Henry exclaimed. "It's my birthday. I was born on this very day in 1926. I'm nineteen. And thanks to you, I am now reborn!" Out of astonishment and joy Henry embraced the young soldier as he laughed and cried at the same time. He looked out into the forest—past his fellow survivors, beyond the U.S. soldiers and their tanks, and into the trees. A flock of birds suddenly flew out and disappeared into the sky as Henry looked on. The smell of the fresh cool air filled Henry's nostrils as he took his first deep breaths of freedom for the first time in many years.

Chapter 9
Revenge

HAVING SURVIVED THE MASSACRE OF THOUSANDS OF HIS fellow prisoners by German soldiers, Henry was brought to a displaced persons camp in Munich, and after being there for only a few days, a group of American GI's started handing out handguns and rifles to some of the Jewish survivors in Henry's group. The U.S. soldiers that liberated Henry were shocked and genuinely appalled at what they witnessed—mass killings, human experimentation, planned starvation, cremation ovens.

"All of the Germans are guilty," one soldier exclaimed.

"They stood by and did nothing to help you. How could they not know what was going on in those camps?" another interjected.

"You should go while you can and get even," another soldier encouraged them.

"Kill as many of them as you can. You'll feel better," advised another as he handed them a weapon.

Henry's small group of men agreed and followed the soldiers as they headed to vehicles to drive them into town. Henry himself was hesitant. He didn't share the same sentiment. He didn't feel that it was right to take revenge on innocent German citizens. He also still didn't know the fate of his family members. As he had no idea who was alive and who wasn't, how could he take revenge for something he wasn't even sure was done? However, not wanting to seem like a coward and being strongly persuaded by his fellow survivors, he started along with the group even though he himself didn't have a gun.

While walking toward the vehicles that would carry Henry and his small vengeful mob into town to exact revenge, he spotted his older cousin Leon, with whom he had shared so much time throughout his long ordeal. He was standing outside a small building and was noticeably distraught. His face was contorted and he was crying bitterly while speaking. He was holding a pistol in one hand, and when he saw Henry, he called out to him. Henry ran over to Leon and asked what was wrong. "I have no reason to live now that she's gone," he moaned. "Hennek, those Nazi bastards killed my wife. Why did I survive? I don't want to live." He held the gun up to his head but Henry reached over to stop him. "Wait. Wait, Leon," he pleaded. "Please don't. She would not want you to do this. We made it so far together. God only knows why we survived and others did not. You must keep going. Don't dishonor your wife's memory by killing yourself, please," Henry begged. Leon fell to the ground, dropping the gun. Henry held him as he wept. Hot blood rushed to Henry's head like an erupting volcano. Anger welled up inside him as he suddenly stood up in a rage. "Goddam those Nazi bastards!" he screamed. He picked up Leon's pistol and ran back over to the group of men headed to the vehicles. He got in a truck headed for town. "Let's get even, goddammit!" Henry yelled, waving his pistol.

Henry's truck rolled into town and pulled over at a busy area. People were walking the streets, shopping, running errands. U.S. army vehicles were everywhere. Agreeing to meet back in one hour, the men piled out of the back of the truck brandishing their weapons and spread out in different directions. When the German civilians saw them, they began to run away in fear. Henry saw one man in his group run into a shop. He heard him screaming, "This is for my parents, you bastards," as he began firing his weapon. People were screaming and running in all directions and bodies fell to the floor. The man ran out of the shop and into another one. More shots were fired. More bodies fell. Witnessing this massacre Henry was reminded of what the German soldiers tried to do to him just a short while ago, and he felt ashamed that he was going to behave in the same reprehensible manner. He looked around to see if any of the men he came with were watching him while he tossed his pistol into some bushes. Just then a young German man came riding past him on a bicycle, and without hesitation Henry knocked him off his bike. Shocked by the unexpected attack, he fell off his bike as it tumbled to the ground. Before he could get back up, Henry picked up his bicycle and rode off with it. "You're lucky you're still alive," Henry yelled at him, feeling like he had power over someone else for a change. Henry smiled as he thought to himself: "You think I'm like you? No. I'm better than you, you goddam Nazi-lover."

As Henry clumsily rode off on his stolen bicycle he was suddenly overwhelmed with a feeling of freedom and exhilaration. He felt like he could ride forever, fearless and unstoppable. He could do as he pleased for the first time in what seemed like forever. He imagined himself riding off through the German countryside and into Poland. He would arrive at his childhood home in Radom. His parents would greet him at the door and embrace him with tears of affection.

"You've returned, Hennek my son," his father Zygmund would say to him. "Come in, my little boychik," his mother Ida would lovingly beckon. "My God, look how you've grown! You're so skinny, though!—Here, eat," she would insist as she sat him down at the dining table. To his surprise and joy all his siblings would be there as well. His older brothers Joe, Harry, and Julius would get up and embrace him. "Can you believe it, Hennek?" Julius would ask. "We all made it and we're back together again." His older sister Celina would come into the room to greet him with her long beautiful hair made up into neat curls perched just perfectly on her head. Her stunning blue eyes, welling up with tears of joy, would stare into his eyes with disbelief. "Are you a ghost?" she would jokingly ask as everyone laughed together. "No, it's really me," Henry would shyly reply as he pinched himself to demonstrate to everyone that he was indeed real.

Little Chaim and Avram would be seated there just as he remembered them. Their feet, too short to reach the ground, would be dangling in front of them and moving back and forth as if they were wading near the side wall inside a swimming pool. "What took you so long?" Chaim would ask in a toddler's broken voice. "I rode here on my bicycle," Henry would reply kneeling down beside him. "It's not easy riding over mountains and through forests, you know." Everyone would laugh.

His older sister Sala would also be there and would get up from the table to greet him as well. She would be wearing that white woolen jacket with the long collar that tied into a bow that he remembered so well. Her hair would be just how he last saw it: short, thick, and wavy, with bangs that stopped just above her perfectly groomed eyebrows and her large, hazel eyes which would be glazed over with tears of happiness. "Welcome home, little brother," she would say while embracing him. Zygmund would hold a long bread knife over the challah while reciting the bracha (blessing). Afterward he would ask Henry to say the prayer over the wine. While holding up his glass Henry would begin: "Barukh ata Adonai, Eloheinu melekh ha'olam, borei p'ri hagafen." ("Blessed are You, Lord our God, ruler of the universe, who creates the fruit of the vine.") Everyone would reply, "Amen." They would all enjoy a home-cooked meal of pot roast with carrots and onions. Bowls with borscht and cooked potatoes would be served, and for dessert there would be Ida's famous rugelach pastry (small twisted cookies). They would recount their stories of survival to one another while gorging themselves with their mother's delicious meal until they could eat no more.

Henry then heard a car horn nearby. He looked to his left and saw a truck coming toward him. Realizing that he had been daydreaming, he found himself in the middle of the street facing an oncoming vehicle. He tried to swerve out of the way, and as he did so he lost control of the bicycle while narrowly avoiding being hit. He tried to stay upright, but the bicycle fell over and crashed into the sidewalk, throwing Henry onto the ground. Luckily he was only slightly bruised. Leaving the bicycle behind, he picked himself up and headed back to the truck that had dropped him off.

When Henry returned to his truck, one of the men from his group shouted to him: "How many did you get, kid? I lost count myself." "Just one," Henry answered. "That's good enough for me." The rest of the men gradually returned to the truck. Many of them were weeping, their faces buried in their hands out of regret, shame, and personal loss. As the truck pulled away Henry stared out of an opening in the canvas canopy and caught a glimpse of the bicycle which he had abandoned. Its owner was happily picking it up and checking it for damage. As the young man rode off on his reclaimed bicycle, Henry smirked to himself feeling relieved that his own guilt didn't involve bullets and blood; just a man's pride and his bike. He knew that what he really wanted even more than revenge was to find the rest of his family. The only thing that mattered to him now was learning what their fate was. He had to know who was still alive and who had perished.

Chapter 10
The Journey Home

As Henry sat in his barrack looking out into the displaced persons (DP) camp that he was temporarily being held at, he had only one thought in his mind—"Who from my family has survived?" At this point in time he had no idea that more than three million of his fellow Jews from Poland were murdered. The Jewish population of Poland before the war was roughly 3.5 million. Less than ten percent survived the Nazi genocide. What he did know, and found hard to believe, was that he was alive, and free. Now it was up to him to decide what to do with the rest of his life. He would decide where to live and what kind of work he would do to make a living. He had just turned 19 years old on the very same day that he was liberated by American GI's. He was reborn from the womb of hell into the arms of freedom, and his first order of business was to find the remaining members of his family.

The United Nations Refugee Relief Agency, otherwise known as UNRRA, set up an office at the center of the DP camp. They gave Henry a temporary passport that allowed him free travel to anywhere within Europe. After a couple of months of recuperating and telling his story to the UNRRA workers and American GI's, Henry set out for his hometown of Radom, Poland. He was told that if anyone from his family had survived, they would most likely go there first. On his way to Poland, Henry stopped in Prague, Czechoslovakia. He travelled by bus and train and was carrying all of his life's possessions in a small, badly worn leather suitcase.

It had only been a short time since the fighting ended in Prague. The devastation was palpably visible. Bombed-out buildings, abandoned military vehicles, and debris were everywhere. When Henry came into town he stopped in front of a large makeshift chalkboard. On it were dozens of names handwritten by survivors. Next to the names were addresses letting separated family members know where they were staying. He started reading down the list, hoping to find a familiar name. To his utter astonishment the name Herschel Koperwas appeared on the board. "Oh my God," he exclaimed, "that's my brother!" He was overwhelmed with joy and excitement. Next to his brother's name was an address of where he was staying in Prague.

Henry quickly made his way through town to the address of his brother. Filled with anticipation he remembered the last time he saw Harry. It was in Tomaszow just outside Radom over three years ago. They were both building barracks there for German soldiers. He and Harry along with their family were forced to live in the Glinice ghetto. After the liquidation of the ghetto he and Harry were separated and he hadn't seen anyone in his family since that day.

The address took him to a displaced persons camp where there were hundreds of people staying temporarily until they either made contact with other family members or decided to go back to their country of origin. There were many rows of small buildings, and when Henry arrived at Harry's door he set his suitcase down and knocked. His heart was racing and he nervously rubbed his sweating palms together as he waited for a reply. The door opened. "Herschel!" exclaimed Henry with a huge smile on his face. Harry's face lit up with amazement. "Haskel!" he exclaimed. "You're alive. I can't believe it." They embraced each other and jumped up and down together while laughing like madmen. Henry never thought he would see any of his family again. Now that he was with his brother, a sense of hope filled his being as he and Harry carried on like giddy children.

"Come inside," Harry beckoned in Yiddish. "Did you come alone?"

"Yes. Just me and my satchel," he replied, bending over to pick up his suitcase. "I can't believe you're alive. What about the rest? Have you found anyone else?" "Yes, Yasel (Joe) and Julius," he responded happily as Henry's eyes beamed with joy and excitement. "Come in and I'll tell you all about it."

Henry walked into Harry's small room and set his suitcase down. Harry went into the tiny kitchen and brought out some cookies and fruit and set them down on a small table. There was a cot next to the window and little else in the room.

"So how did you hear about our brothers Julius and Yasel? Where are they?" Henry asked.

"Julius is in Krakow," Harry began. "He's married to a girl named Basha and they have a son named Ygnaz. This whole time he was in Russia posing as a Russian soldier. Can you believe it? He actually fought in the Russian army!"

"That's unbelievable," Henry replied with laughter. "On that day when he drove off with his boss when we were all living at Kilinskiego 11 in Radom, I thought that I would never see him again. Where did you meet him?"

"In Radom. He left a note at our old place."

"And what about Yasel?" Henry inquired.

"He's in Germany in Breslau. He's married to a beautiful lady named Regina."

"What about the rest? Any word?" Henry asked with a saddened tone. He wasn't very hopeful about his parents, sisters, or little brothers. He had always assumed that they didn't last very long, yet he was still somehow hoping for a miracle.

Harry bit his lower lip while looking down at the ground. "There's very little chance that any of them survived," he said with a lowered voice. "The first place they would've gone would be our house in Radom, but they left no note. If our little brothers Chaim or Avram survived, their names would be on file with one of the organizations. I checked them all; there's nothing."

"How could they have made it?" Henry asked. "The Nazis probably killed them right away, those bastards!"

Henry then remembered the last time he saw his parents. It was when they got separated from him the night the ghetto was liquidated almost four years ago. In the commotion and chaos, he watched as his father joined his mother and his two little brothers on a different line. He looked on helplessly as they disappeared into the crowd, never to be seen again. He wished he could go back to that day and change the course of events. He felt that perhaps, knowing what he knows now, he could have saved them.

"By the way, I'm going to Palestine," Harry interjected, changing the subject. "It's more important now than ever before that our people have a homeland where we can decide our future for ourselves so that this never happens again. No more Nazi bastards or anyone else will ever tell me what to do again." Henry could hear the anger and conviction in his voice.

"What, you're going to live on a kibbutz now?" Henry responded disapprovingly.

"Who said anything about a kibbutz? I'll get an apartment," Harry explained. "You think we should stay here? You think, all of a sudden, these people are going to accept us? No, don't kid yourself, they still hate us and wish that Hitler had finished us all off. No, I'm not sticking around here. This can never be our home."

"I'm not saying we should stay here, Herschel," Henry replied. "We should all go to America. There we can start over. I was talking with one Jewish soldier from Brooklyn who I met in Dachau. He told me that life in America is good. No one will bother us there. We can be whatever we want."

"How will you get to America?" Harry asked. "Don't you know that the quota for Polish survivors to go to the U.S. is already filled? The group HIAS (Hebrew Immigrant Aid Society) can't send you there. It's too late. You should come to Palestine with me and help us form a Jewish state," Harry urged.

"I don't want to fight, Herschel. I just want to live my life in peace," Henry replied. "Look, nobody knows where we are from. There are no records. We can tell them we were born in Germany and that we moved to Poland later on. How will they know? Besides, what difference does it make where we were born? It was the Germans who did this to us while the Poles stood around and did nothing, or turned us in for some butter or a loaf of bread. You think I'm going to stay here? No, I agree with you, Herschel. We can't stay here with these Jew-haters. They'll never change!"

"I don't know, Haskel," Harry replied while lighting a cigarette. "Let's talk to Julius and Yasel and see what they think."

"Alright," Henry agreed. "Let's see what they have to say. You said that Julius is in Krakow, right?"

"Yeah, he's waiting for his wife and little boy to come from Russia."

"Okay. Why don't I go to Krakow and bring Julius and his family back here? Then we can all go to Germany and meet up with Yasel and his wife in Breslau," Henry suggested.

"Sure, Haskel, sure," Harry agreed. "Let's all get together and decide what to do."

They ate a little food together and told each other stories of survival. Henry slept on the floor on some blankets. The next morning, he left some of his personal belongings with Harry and set off to meet his older brother Julius in Krakow.

When Henry arrived in Krakow he was amazed at how little of the city was damaged. Unlike other Polish cities like Warsaw, Poznan, and Bialystok, which were virtually razed to the ground, Krakow was practically untouched. He saw a few bombed-out roads and bridges on his way into town, but the overwhelming majority of the city appeared to be from another world. Henry particularly noticed the shining windows, flawless paved roads, and perfectly intact rooftops. People were walking through the streets wearing nice clothing, right down to their shoes. He wondered how this city had escaped the destruction of the war.

Just a short while ago Krakow was liberated from the Nazis by the USSR's Red Army. In 1939 it was proclaimed the capital of the General Government, a new territory created and governed by Nazi Germany. As such, Krakow served as the Third Reich's supply base during the war and therefore was an important part of the Nazi army's infrastructure that was valued and preserved by them. The Nazis even gave Krakow the title of Urdeutsche Stadt ("old German city"), and did everything in their power to Germanize the inhabitants. They imposed totalitarian rule, sending Polish intellectuals and scholars to concentration camps and engaging in the systematic extermination of the Jews there.

After the Russians liberated the city, Henry's brother Julius, along with his wife Basha and their small son Ygnaz, made their way to Krakow from Russia. Henry hadn't seen Julius since he left home in Radom to go to Russia with his employer over six years ago. He had no idea what had happened to him and was thrilled to be meeting him again after such a long time and after so much struggle.

Henry arrived at Julius and Basha's apartment by midday. He knocked on the door anxiously, and when it opened he was greeted by a tall beautiful woman whom he had never met. "Can I help you?" she asked him in Polish. She was wearing a colorful blouse and a wool skirt that fell just above her knees. Her long brunette hair was partially pulled back and held in place with a hair clip. Her bright hazel eyes were offset by her smooth, clear complexion.

"You must be Basha. I'm Julius's brother Hennek," he replied.

"Oh my God! Yeedal," she called out in Polish to Julius. "It's your brother Hennek—come quickly!"

Julius quickly came out of the next room. "Haskela, Haskela, oh my God, I can't believe it's you!" he shouted while running over to hug his little brother. "Look at you, you're all grown up now. The last time I saw you, you were this tall," he said holding his right hand up to the lower part of his chest. "Oh my God," he exclaimed again while continuing to hug Henry.

Basha then went into the next room and brought their little boy out cradled in her arms. "This is your nephew Ygnaz," she said beaming with a joyous smile.

Henry walked over and greeted his first nephew. He was a cute, little two-year-old with long blonde hair, large blue eyes, and full, chubby cheeks. Henry greeted him with typical baby talk and a large smile. Basha suggested that they all go for a walk downtown with Ygnaz, and that way they could show Henry the city and chat with one another. Basha pulled out a small baby carriage from a closet and put on a blazer that matched her skirt. Julius grabbed a coat and they all headed out.

Basha showed Henry all the nearby restaurants and shops while he and Julius told each other their stories of how they managed to survive and all the terrible things which they witnessed. They stopped at a photographer's studio and took some pictures together. Henry was repeatedly amazed that Krakow was such a beautiful city and that it was untouched by the war. He felt lucky to be alive and in the company of his brother again, along with his wife and their son, his nephew. Eventually they headed back to the apartment. While they enjoyed each other's company they all decided they would go back to Prague to meet Harry and then all go together to Breslau to meet up with Henry's other older brother Joe and his wife Regina. Henry stayed with them for a few days while they made arrangements to leave for Prague.

*   *   *   *   *

A few months later, Henry and his three brothers along with their wives and his one nephew were all together for the first time in Breslau, which was now called Wroclaw. Most of the German inhabitants were leaving or being forced out of the city and were being resettled in either the Soviet or allied occupation zones. For most of the war Wroclaw remained untouched. Unfortunately, toward the end of the war half of the city was destroyed and nearly 40,000 civilians were killed in the Battle of Breslau which lasted three months when the Soviet Red Army laid siege to the city.

Many Holocaust survivors from Poland had moved to Wroclaw after the war. There had been a Jewish community there for several centuries, but after the war only one synagogue remained called the Storch. Most of the Jews who previously lived there were killed in concentration camps, yet now many Jews had returned and established a community there. The German government gave Henry and his brothers a place to live.

One evening Henry and his brother Joe along with his wife Regina and their friend Benyek decided to go to a nearby pub to celebrate. Joe bought drinks for everyone. They stood at the bar telling each other stories in Yiddish about their survival. Henry had just put down his drink after taking a sip and laughing along with Joe and Regina when a group of five Polish men about the same age as Henry walked over to them. The mood changed quickly.

"Hey, verflucht Juden. What are you doing in here?" one of them asked angrily. He knew they were Jewish from the Yiddish they spoke.

Henry's blood began to boil. That term reminded him of the time he was forced to march in the streets, half-starved, on his way to Dachau. A small boy used that same exact expression while hurling a stone at him. Now that he was free he would not tolerate any more abuse.

"Verflucht Juden?" Henry replied defensively. "Yes, we're Jews, but we're not verflucht (accursed)! We're having a drink and enjoying ourselves like everyone else."

Joe leaned in holding out his arm. "Henry, it's okay. There are five of them. Calm down," he urged his younger brother in Yiddish.

"Verflucht? These bastards are just like the Hitler Youth; they're brainwashed to hate us. I've had it," Henry said as anger filled his face. He pushed Joe's arm away. He was ready to fight.

The man then pulled out a knife and pointed it at Henry. "Listen, you don't belong here, you filthy Jew. Hitler may not have killed you, but you will not be so lucky with us," he threatened while looking down at his knife.

"Why don't you guys just leave us alone since we're not bothering you?" asked Benyek.

"Let's go, c'mon," Regina commanded nervously as she dragged Joe and Henry by their arms and headed for the door. Benyek followed behind.

Just before Benyek got out of the door, one of the men grabbed him by the shoulder and spun him around.

Another man punched him in the face while another hit him in the stomach. Regina screamed as Joe and Henry pulled him away, pushing the men back, and then they all ran for their lives. As they fled down the street, cries of "Verflucht Juden!" spewed from the young men. "Run, you diseased Jews. Run. Get out!"

After this incident Henry knew that he could never fit into German or Polish society as a Jew; he would always be an outsider. People would either look at him as a helpless victim in need of their sympathy, or as one deserving of what happened—one who didn't get the message and was not welcome and who needed to leave. Both views were unacceptable. In Henry's mind the war might be over, but his struggle was not. German and Polish society still regarded the Jew as a problem, as someone who was neither fully German nor fully Polish. Henry looked at every person he met with suspicion and contempt. He was always thinking: "What were you doing during the war? Where were your parents? Were they working for the Nazis? Were they turning Jews over to the Gestapo (organized secret police)? Were they stealing Jews' property and belongings? Do you think that I'm an Untermenschen, a subhuman?"

He realized that he could never live in peace in this place. German nationalism led to the near extermination of his people. German nationalism fueled by anti-Semitism left Henry crawling away from death on his belly in the snow, under the hail of machine gun fire aimed by soldiers full of hate for the Jew. The German people took his home, his family, and his adolescent years, but they were not going to take away his dignity. He had to get away and completely start over. He had to remake himself on the ground of a new land.

For Henry, the answer to the Jewish question in Europe was to leave and go where he would not stand out; someplace where he would not be forced to wear his Jewishness on his sleeve; a place where he could choose what to wear and when; a place where no separate laws applied only to him and his kind, restricting which professions he could work in and which ones he could not, and where there were no special taxes imposed on him for being Jewish; a place where he could live wherever he chose or walk on whatever side of the street he wanted to. For him that place was clearly America, a land which would not treat him differently because he was a Jew. That was a land where he could be both a Jew and a citizen with equal rights under the law. Henry found it hard to believe that such a place even existed, but he knew that it did; the American GI's who liberated him assured him of this, and he believed them. Now he was convinced more than ever that he had no alternative but to go there.

Henry discussed with his brothers how he felt about going to America, and told them that since the quota set for Polish Jews emigrating to America was full, the only way that any of them could get there was to tell the German government that they were born in Germany and that their family moved to Poland when they were small children. Since they were born at home and because there were no official documents remaining after the war, they just needed to report a town and street number to the German officials. Henry learned that the town of Dortmund was badly damaged during the war. Many of the residential areas were bombed out and lay in ruins. He reasoned that this would be the perfect place to claim as his birth town. He used his free train pass to travel to Dortmund from Munich.

One of the largest enterprises in the capitalist world at the time was the Deutsche Reichsbahn, the German National Railway. It was an elaborate state-run railway system that played two significant roles during the war. First, it had an important logistic function in supporting the rapid movement of German troops, tanks, and supplies throughout Germany and to the occupied territories as well.

Secondly, this enormous railway system made it possible to transport large numbers of Jews from their home towns and cities to various Nazi camps throughout Germany and Poland. In other words, without the mass transportation provided by the Deutsche Reichsbahn, the scale of the "Final Solution" would not have been possible.

Henry had experienced in full living horror the agony of being packed into a guterwagen, a boxcar for transporting cattle, on his way to Auschwitz just a few years earlier. While he now sat in comfort staring out of the window of the train on his way to Dortmund, he remembered how he, along with about two hundred others, were packed into a single car that could barely fit fifty people. Devoid of seats, food, or water, he remembered the stench of the single bucket that served as the latrine, the lack of light, the inability to move or sit, and the fear and desperation in peoples' faces as loved ones, friends, and relatives suffocated while standing. Now, he rode in relative luxury as he looked around the cabin wondering what all of the German passengers on board did during the war. "Was that man one of the soldiers that forced me into a boxcar? ...What about that one? ...Or him over there—was he one of the guards at Auschwitz or Unterriexingen?" Henry couldn't keep from asking himself these questions. He viewed all Germans as guilty in one way or another because in his mind they either actively cooperated with the Nazis or they lent their silent approval by passively ignoring what was happening. "There will never be a good German," Henry thought to himself. "Never!"

As he was scanning the passengers and holding them accountable for what had happened to him, he noticed an attractive young woman about his age staring at him.

She was riding alone and looked away when Henry's eyes caught hers. Noticing that Henry was sitting by himself, she got up from her seat and shyly walked toward him. Henry couldn't help noticing how pretty she was. She smilingly introduced herself and asked Henry where he was going. Perhaps she had heard that many Jewish survivors were riding the trains in search of their relatives and thought that Henry could use some help. He hesitatingly told her that he was heading to Dortmund to find the home that he was born in. She told him that she was from Dortmund and was heading back home after visiting her boyfriend. She eagerly offered to help and asked Henry to come meet her father when they arrived in Dortmund. She seemed genuinely concerned about what had happened to Henry and his family after hearing his story. She invited him to come to her home for lunch and insisted that her father would be happy to help him obtain a German birth certificate. Henry was surprised by this. He had just condemned all Germans of being complicit in Nazi atrocities. "Could it be that some people were opposed to what the Nazis were doing?" he thought to himself. "Maybe her family felt that what the Nazis were doing was wrong but they just had no way of doing anything about it." He gladly accepted the young woman's invitation and spent the rest of the train ride telling her his story. When the train arrived in

Dortmund her father was waiting to pick her up. Henry accompanied them to their home.

After a modest meal the German man and his daughter offered to drive Henry wherever he needed to go. Henry had heard that large parts of Dortmund were bombed during the war and that entire neighborhoods were reduced to piles of rubble. He asked his newly-found hosts to take him to one of those bombed-out areas.

Standing amidst the ruins, he picked a street to be the place of his birth: Rauschbergstrasse. They all got back in the car and went to a government building to apply for a German birth certificate. To Henry's surprise, by the end of the day he was holding his birth certificate in his hands. He wondered how many times he would have to be "reborn" before he could get to America. He considered the day of his liberation—May 1st, 1945, which coincided with his actual birthday—to be his second birth. Now, looking down at the document in his hand, he felt as though he was reborn again, and this time he was certain that it would bring him closer to his goal of reaching America. He thanked the young woman and her father and wasted no time in getting back to Munich to finish registering with the officials there.

While Henry waited for his approval to come from the German government he moved to Neufahrn, a few miles northeast of Munich. There he started playing soccer again and eventually joined a professional team.

He wished that his father was able to watch him play. He always remembered the night when his father told him that one day he would be playing in a large stadium. It was as if his father had prophesied this very moment. Every time Henry would score a goal he would imagine his father rising to his feet, clapping his hands, and cheering him on. Knowing that could never happen made Henry angry and caused him to play more ferociously. He wanted to prove to the German people that he wasn't only as good as them; he was better!

A few months later Henry was riding in a small bus on his way to the nearby port of Bremerhaven where he would board a ship to America. After a short ride he got out of the bus carrying everything which he owned in the world: a small leather suitcase, his boarding ticket, and twenty-four U.S. dollars which he kept in his wallet along with his identification papers. A short while ago he said farewell to his three brothers Joe, Julius, and Harry, and was hopeful that he would soon see them all again in America. Now Henry stood at the embarkation dock in front of the SS Marine Marlin. He paused for a brief moment with a feeling of gratitude to the HIAS organization for arranging his passage to America. Looking down at the boarding ticket, he proceeded toward the ship.

The SS Marine Marlin was built in 1945 by Kaiser Shipyards in Vancouver, Washington, as a troop transport ship with the capacity to carry over 3000 troops when it was operated by the U.S. War Shipping Administration. Just a year ago she was chartered to the transatlantic shipping company called the United States Lines and fitted to carry almost 1000 tourist-class passengers. Now she was being used to transport refugees and immigrants to America, and Henry, along with a few hundred other survivors, were lucky enough to be taking the 10-day journey across the Atlantic to New York.

Henry's hopes were high. Even though he had lost most of his family, he still had his three brothers and now he had the opportunity of starting over in the richest country in the world. "Are the streets really lined with gold?" he naively thought to himself. "Will I be greeted as a hero, with people surrounding me and asking me to recount my tale of survival?" Henry anxiously walked up the narrow stairs leading to the ship's deck and was greeted by the captain. "Welcome aboard," the captain said cheerfully as Henry handed him his ticket. Henry felt the ship slightly swaying on the water. He had never been on a large seaworthy vessel before. He realized that soon he would be on his way across the Atlantic and landing in New York City, where he could firmly place his feet on the ground in his new home and have a fresh start in life.

After setting his few belongings in his cabin, Henry stood on the main deck as the ship pulled out of port.

As he watched the small town of Bremerhaven shrink behind him and fade into the coastline, he knew that he would never, ever be back. He recalled that night at Kilinskiego 11 when he was just 13 years old. He had just come in from playing soccer with his friends. He was holding his football under his arm as he kissed his father goodnight. His father patted him on the head, assuring him that tomorrow would be a better day. Henry felt that his tomorrow had finally come. He raised his voice at the distant shore and shouted, "I'm still alive, you Nazi bastards. Go to hell, all of you!" He turned with a smile on his face as he made his way back to his quarters, never looking back.

The Beginning

Epilogue

HENRY ARRIVED IN NEW YORK ON JULY 17, 1945. He began working in the garment industry as a tailor while attending night school to learn English. After a few years he successfully started his own business manufacturing ladies' outerwear, commonly known in Jewish circles as the "schmatta" business. He retired after 35 years.

Henry met his wife Norma at a dance in Brooklyn. They were married on December 11, 1954. Together they raised three children in Long Island, NY. They are still happily married and currently live in Tamarac, Florida. Henry is 92 years old and Norma is 83. They have nine grandchildren.

Success is the best revenge!

About the Author

Mark Koperweis is co-founder and Executive Director of the Henry Koperweis Foundation for Holocaust Education, a non-profit organization dedicated to educating the public about the atrocities committed by the Nazis against the Jews of Europe.

He lives in Oakland, California, where he owns and operates a successful window coverings business—draperyGuru®.

This is his first book, compiled from hours of recorded interviews with his father Henry—the subject of this memoir.

To learn more please visit:
www.henrykoperweisfoundation.org